100
SLOPES
OF A LIFETIME

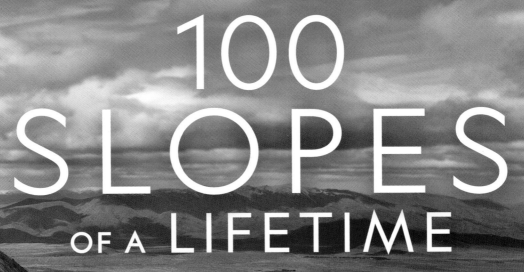

100
SLOPES
OF A LIFETIME

*The World's Ultimate Ski
and Snowboard Destinations*

GORDY MEGROZ

FOREWORD BY LINDSEY VONN

NATIONAL GEOGRAPHIC

WASHINGTON, D.C.

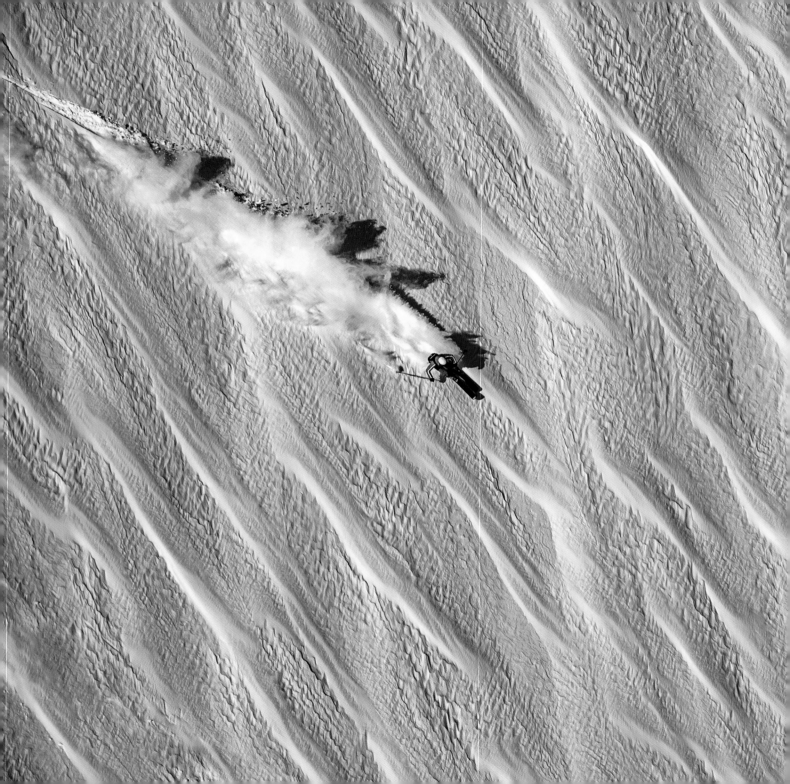

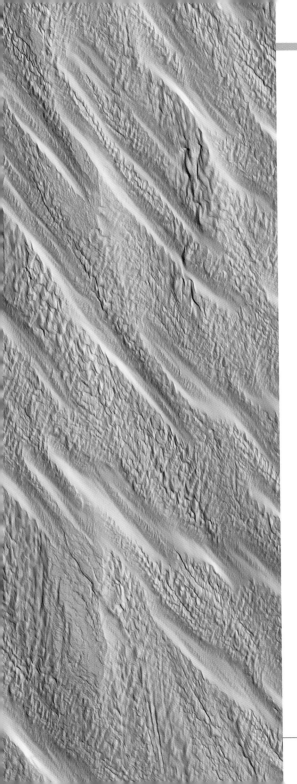

CONTENTS

LEFT: A skier carves fresh tracks into new powder at Åre Ski Area in Sweden (p. 242).

PAGES 2-3: Located on New Zealand's South Island, skiers find expansive views of Lake Ahau from the slopes of the Ahau skifield.

FOREWORD

It might surprise you to know that I didn't fall in love with skiing right off the bat. Growing up in Minnesota, my first memory of skiing wasn't the adrenaline rush, it was that it was really, really cold. My dad got me on skis early in my childhood, around two years old, on a teeny, tiny hill called Buck Hill. My dad was a junior national champion ski racer and hoped I would follow in his footsteps, but the only way he could get me on the hill was by promising me hot chocolate and glazed donuts afterwards. As I got older—and my blood got thicker—I began falling in love with the sport (even though I still love a good après-ski with hot chocolate and donuts). There was one trail that really helped shift my perspective—my first favorite trail.

I started ski racing when I was seven, and we'd train at Buck Hill at night. During training, I'd sneak off and ski an unofficial run off the backside of the ski area. I loved it because there were two mini jumps that I'd hit. I probably didn't get very much air, but I felt like I was flying. It's hard not to become addicted to that feeling—whether you're jumping off something, floating through powder, or even gliding fast across a groomed trail—you become weightless and give in to the mountain.

Over the years, there were more trails that I fell in love with, both because I enjoyed the terrain and because I adored experiencing the culture, food, and customs they brought me to. There were the courses on the World Cup, full of big jumps and fast, sweeping turns, that made you feel like you were driving at top speed with your head out the window. When the tour would stop in Austria or Switzerland, I'd *rodelbahn*—a form of tobogganing down these long, banked trails—drink *gluhwein*, and eat *kaiserschmarrn*, a thick, eggy pancake with raisins, powdered sugar, and lots of butter (it's my favorite food).

There was the time I went heli-skiing in British Columbia. I was 16 and had never really skied off-piste before. We stayed in little cabins and explored

these beautiful untouched mountains, skiing down endless runs with bottomless powder. And there were the trails I skied in New Zealand, moderately pitched descents with jagged, towering rocks jutting out of the slopes around you. After skiing, we'd go down the mountain and play golf or bungee jump among rolling green hills and flocks of sheep.

And that's what I enjoy most about *100 Slopes of a Lifetime*—a celebration of the variety of ski and snowboard trails (and the world that surrounds them) at our fingertips. This book has 100 trails in it, located all over the world, that offer the types of experiences that I've been lucky enough to enjoy—and more. In these pages, you'll find everything from easy groomers with mind-blowing views; to open bowls full of light, deep powder; to steep couloirs. And you'll get a taste of the culture, cuisine, and history of the areas where they're located. As you flip through it, I hope you find all the inspiration you need for your next ski or snowboard trip. Happy trails!

—Lindsey Vonn, FEBRUARY 2021

Lindsey Vonn celebrates her bronze medal win at the women's downhill event during the Pyeongchang 2018 Winter Olympic Games in South Korea.

INTRODUCTION

I f you're like me, and I'm guessing a lot of you who are reading this book are (we're all skiers and snowboarders, right?), then you probably spent your formative years on the slopes mostly going to one ski area, where you had a favorite trail. I was lucky enough to grow up 10 miles (16.1 km) from Stratton Mountain, a ski area in southern Vermont. For me, the trail was Liftline. Bordered by snow-caked pines, spruce, beech, and maples on either side, the trail has a consistent 25- to 30-degree pitch, some swooping bends, a big waterfall drop, and, if you're so inclined, a lip that's perfect for hitting with speed and taking flight, views of the rolling Green Mountains in front of you as you soar through the air. As a kid, I took every opportunity I could to ski that slope, carving my edges through perfectly groomed corduroy during early morning runs or sloshing through mounds of corn snow on warm afternoons in the springtime. I thought Liftline had it all. Then I went skiing in Utah.

Out West, I discovered bowls full of powder, steep couloirs, and tree lines that went on forever. I developed a love for moguls, which, when they're not icy, are really quite enjoyable. Over the years, I've had the good fortune to ski all over the world. In Japan, where it seemingly never stops snowing, I found a trail that descended through trees that looked as if they were coated in vanilla icing and ended in front of a tiny bar that served locally distilled whiskey. In Alaska, I learned what the big fuss was about heli-skiing. I flew deep into the mountains and looked out at boats bobbing on the Cook Inlet as I descended spines and glaciated powder runs that went on for 4,000 vertical feet (1,219.2 m). I liked the trails in Jackson Hole, Wyoming, so much that I have made it my home.

I still have a lot of love for Liftline, but in the 43 years that I've been skiing, the thing that I've discovered is that there are thousands of incredible runs all over this planet—and I still haven't been down most of them. That point was hammered home when I was researching this book. I reached out to

ABOVE: **Catch great powder turns—and a stunning golden glow—in the late afternoon sun at La Parva Ski Resort in Chile (p. 260).**

PAGES 10-11: **A chairlift climbs through the clouds at Killington Ski Resort in Killington, Vermont (p. 186).**

professional skiers and snowboarders, guides, instructors and patrollers, and other ski and snowboard journalists, and I kept finding myself saying, "Oh, that's gotta be in the book."

In the end, I narrowed it down to 100 spectacular slopes, some of them special because they're so challenging, others because they offer a unique cultural experience—like eating an authentic Italian meal in a tiny hut halfway down the trail (p. 240)—and others because they offer the ultimate viewpoint to astonishing scenery. Quite a few encapsulate all three aspects. For example, at Hapat Khued Bowl (p. 262), a trail at Gulmarg Ski Area in India, you can drink mint tea, eat a bowl of curry, and look out at the peaks of the Himalaya before descending a 36-degree slope for more than 3,000 feet (914.4 m).

As you read, you'll probably recognize well-known trails like Jackson Hole's Corbet's Couloir (p. 312), Goat at Stowe Mountain Resort (p. 182), and Vallée

Blanche in France (p. 62). Some of the trails are old—people have been skiing down the slopes at New Hampshire's Tuckerman Ravine (p. 304) for more than 100 years—and some are very new: Just a few years ago, the trail that will host the downhill event at the 2022 Winter Olympics in China didn't even exist (p. 338).

There are also destinations in this book where you might never have known ski areas existed, like Oukaïmeden (p. 252), a resort in Morocco with just one chairlift. As I was writing about Oukaïmeden, I was surprised to find out that despite it being the warmest continent on Earth, there are even a handful of ski areas in Africa.

In fact, though I've written extensively about snow sports for various magazines for close to 20 years, as I was working on *100 Slopes of a Lifetime* I realized there was still a lot I didn't know about skiing and snowboarding. Were you aware, for example, that one person, a Frenchman named Émile Allais, was responsible for creating several of the world's most beloved trails? Or that there are meteorological and geographical factors that help support the claim printed on Utah's license plate: "Greatest Snow on Earth"? Or that the first machine used specifically for grooming alpine ski trails was invented in Winter Park, Colorado?

I hope that as you read, you'll be as captivated by the history, culture, and terrain of these slopes as I was while writing about them—and that this book will make you want to go ski some of these trails yourself. I hope to see you out there.

PART ONE

INTERMEDIATE

The town of Vail sparkles beneath the mountains as the sun sets over Vail Valley, Colorado.

ARIZONA SNOWBOWL

Must-Try Trail: Upper and Lower Ridge to Phoenix to Agassiz

MAX ELEVATION: 11,500 feet (3,505.2 m) **AVERAGE SNOWFALL:** 260 inches (660.4 cm)
SKIABLE TERRAIN: 777 acres (314.4 ha) **OPEN SKI SEASON:** Mid-November through April

Imagine this: You're skiing down a moderately pitched trail for 2,000 vertical feet (609.6 m), the entire way taking in panoramic views of the snow-spackled ochre mesas of the Grand Canyon's North Rim. That's possible only at the Arizona Snowbowl, an 83-year-old ski area located in northern Arizona's San Francisco Peaks—and it's only one of the unique landscapes skiers can see as they carve down the mountain. To the south are the city of Flagstaff and the Mogollon Rim, a 200-mile-long (321.9 km) escarpment with 200-foot-high white sandstone cliffs. To the north is the Kachina Peaks Wilderness, more than 18,000 acres (7,284.3 ha) of mountains and forests that include Humphrey's Peak, which, at 12,633 feet (3,850.5 m), is the highest mountain in Arizona.

The best way to take in all this scenery is by skiing the Upper Ridge-Lower Ridge-Phoenix-Agassiz linkup, a series of trails that starts just above the tree line, at the very top of the 11,500-foot (3,505.2 m) ski area, and descends all the way to the base of the mountain. Views aside, the trails, which are lined with gnarled bristlecone pines and meander down a ridgeline on the western face of the mountain, will also appeal to any level skier.

"Ski it in the afternoon," advises Sven Brunso, a professional skier who once called the Snowbowl his home mountain. "It's west facing, so if you ski it right at the end of the day, it's like you're skiing right into the sun."

APRÈS SKI

Continue to enjoy Arizona's setting sun on the large west-facing deck of the Hart Prairie Lodge. Located at the base of the mountain, the lodge's bar serves nachos and personal pizzas as well as locally brewed beer. Advises Brunso, "Relax and let the traffic go down the hill, away from the ski area, before you try to make your way down or you'll just be sitting in a line of traffic."

Arizona Snowbowl is home to 2,300 feet (701 m) of vertical drop and offers plenty of fresh powder in the Southwest.

HEAVENLY MOUNTAIN RESORT

Must-Try Trail: Ridge Run

MAX ELEVATION: 10,067 feet (3,068.4 m) **AVERAGE SNOWFALL:** 360 inches (914.4 cm)
SKIABLE TERRAIN: 4,800 acres (1,942.5 ha) **OPEN SKI SEASON:** Mid-November through April

The toughest part about skiing Ridge Run, a solidly intermediate trail at Heavenly Mountain Resort, is staying focused on what you're doing. The entire 1,600-vertical-foot (487.7 m) run looks out at Lake Tahoe, a hypnotic, nearly 200-square-mile (518 sq km) aquamarine distraction that shimmers in the near distance. "People will often say, 'I almost crashed because I was looking at the view,'" says Mike Allen, director of skier services at Heavenly.

The trail has a long history of breaking skiers' concentration. The ski area, which straddles the Nevada/California border in the Sierra Nevada, opened in 1955, and Ridge Run was one of the resort's original trails. It's so named because it wends from the top of the 10,067-foot (3,068.4 m) mountain down the western ridge of Heavenly's boundary, bordered by Douglas firs and white pines of the Desolation Wilderness.

The wide run with a gentle pitch is one of the first trails to open each year (usually in mid-November), and it stays well covered throughout the season, even during low-snow years. That's thanks to Heavenly's robust snowmaking operation; the ski area employs 230 snowmaking guns, 46 of which line Ridge Run. It's also groomed every night, so early risers with the ability to do so can arc fast turns down a fresh carpet of manicured snow—as long as they can keep their eyes off the lake.

WHERE TO STAY

Founded in 2012, Basecamp Hotel is an old motel that's been refurbished for a chic and modern look. Inside are comfortable guest rooms and a lounge with couches and a fireplace. Outside are fire pits where you can hang out, sip cocktails, or roast s'mores, as well as an Airstream trailer that's set up for business meetings.

Take in the majestic views as you ride Heavenly Mountain Resort's chairlift to the peak.

VAIL SKI RESORT

Must-Try Trail: The Minturn Mile

MAX ELEVATION: 11,570 feet (3,527 m)   **AVERAGE SNOWFALL:** 354 inches (899.2 cm)
SKIABLE TERRAIN: 5,317 acres (2,141 ha)   **OPEN SKI SEASON:** Mid-November to April

Soon after Vail Ski Resort opened in 1962, local skiers discovered a new adventure. They realized that they could ride the lift to the top of the mountain, go on a little hike, exit the ski area, and take a wild, often powder-filled trail into the old mining town of Minturn, where they could kick up their ski boots and enjoy a drink at a nearly 100-year-old saloon. Thus, the Minturn Mile was born.

A few things to know before you go: First, the Minturn Mile trail is not really a mile long (blame the name on alliteration). It's more like 3 or 4 miles long (4.8 or 6.4 km).

Second, the Mile is a backcountry ski run, so you need to carry the appropriate equipment, including a beacon, shovel, and probe. And if you're not comfortable navigating backcountry trails, hire a guide to lead you.

Finally, since getting to the Minturn Mile requires riding a chairlift, you'll need to throw down for a lift ticket at Vail. This isn't a bad thing. That old saloon—the Minturn Saloon—is still serving drinks, but it doesn't open until 3 p.m. So you can enjoy a day of skiing at the resort before heading out the backcountry gate sometime around 2:30.

To access the Minturn Mile trail, ride the Game Creek Express chairlift and then follow the Lost Boy trail to Ptarmigan Ridge. From there, it's a 10-minute hike to the clearly marked backcountry gate. You'll exit the ski area into a

OFF THE SLOPES

Bōl is a modern bowling alley. As you knock down pins, you can snack on upscale dishes like lamb lollipops with chimichurri sauce and ahi tuna poke, while enjoying a creative cocktail, such as Mad Beets: gin, fresh beets, lemon, rhubarb, sugar, and champagne.

OPPOSITE: Extreme skier Kina Pickett carves into Vail's abundant fresh powder.

PAGES 20-21: Vail Village has heated pedestrian streets meant for strolling from shops to restaurants après-ski.

bowl and make 20 or so turns down a 25-degree open slope.

"On a powder day, it's always nice to find a few more soft turns toward the end of the day," says Mike Kloser, an adventure racer, skier, and outdoor gear manufacturer who lives in Vail. "Since it's outside the ski area, it gets a bit less traffic, so you can usually find untouched snow."

At the bottom of the bowl, you'll ski through a glade of pine and aspen trees before reaching the Game Creek drainage, a twisty, turny section of trail that leads up and down sidehills, under low-hanging branches, and over natural terrain features that, if you're so inclined, can be used as jumps. "It's like an adult playground," says Kloser.

After a creek crossing, you arrive at the Mile's most popular section: the luge, a nearly 2-mile (3.2 km) descent through a narrow, natural halfpipe. At times, depending on snow conditions and the time of day you're hitting it, the luge can become icy and fast, and advanced skiers will use this opportunity to open the throttle, trying to

WHERE TO STAY

In 1919, the Faessler family started a hotel in Ofterschwang, Germany, that still exists. Sixty years later, the same family brought their upscale German bed-and-breakfast model to the U.S., starting the Sonnenalp in Vail. Since then, the hotel has become an institution, and is one of the oldest family-run businesses in the region. It has a spa with all the bells and whistles, but the highlight might be its breakfast: a smorgasbord of fresh fruit, eggs, and pastries.

maneuver the gully at high speeds while staying inside the track. (Less confident skiers need not worry: You can safely employ a comfortable snowplow to stay in control.)

The luge exits near Taylor Street, in the town of Minturn, established in 1904, with a current population of just more than 1,000. Unlike its surrounding neighbors, Minturn has stayed true to its historic Colorado roots, and is considered by many the true "hometown" of the Vail area. Here is where you can click off your skis and take a short walk to the Minturn Saloon.

The century-old establishment is considered a landmark in Vail and the area's most historic restaurant. And it fits the part: The saloon is decorated with a bison head, old ski photos and posters, and town memorabilia. Sit by the fireplace, snack on free chips and salsa, and throw back a pitcher of the saloon's famous margaritas.

ABOVE: **On Gondola One at Vail, skiers and snowboarders have Rocky Mountain views on their way to mid-mountain trails.**

OPPOSITE: **Vail's 195 trails offer an abundance of options for all levels of skiers and boarders.**

SILVERTON MOUNTAIN

Must-Try Trail: The Ramp

MAX ELEVATION: 13,487 feet (4,110.8 m)   **AVERAGE SNOWFALL:** 400 inches (1,016 cm)
SKIABLE TERRAIN: 26,819 acres (10,853.6 ha)   **OPEN SKI SEASON:** Late November to April

I n 2001, when Jen and Aaron Brill opened Silverton Mountain, it was vastly different from any other ski area in North America. Situated above a dilapidated mining town in southern Colorado's San Juan Mountains, Silverton rises 13,487 feet (4,110.8 m) above sea level, receives about 400 inches (1,016 cm) of snow each year, and has 26,819 acres (10,853.3 ha)—a large portion accessible only by helicopter—of some of the country's best and most challenging terrain: chutes, bowls, cliff drops, and steep tree skiing.

The mountain, which was dotted with old mining claims, had been scantly skied over the years by backcountry enthusiasts. The Brills bought up all the claims in 1999 to turn the mountain into a sort of backcountry-style ski area. There would be avalanche mitigation work done, but skiers would still need to carry safety equipment, including a transceiver, shovel, and probe, and, except for a few weeks in the spring, they'd be required to ski with a guide. Unlike the ritzy resorts, the Brills would keep things simple: no food services, no fancy chairlifts or lodges, and absolutely no trail grooming.

To that end, the Brills installed a small yurt at the base of the mountain to be used as a warming hut and a single two-seat chairlift (purchased second-hand from Mammoth Mountain) that climbs 1,900 feet (579.1 m) up the mountain. From there, skiers can easily descend a few runs. But to get to the majority of Silverton's 70 or so trails ("We don't keep very good count of how

ALTERNATIVE ROUTE

In 2008, the Brills added helicopter skiing to Silverton. At $179 (plus a lift ticket), this single flight into the backcountry is one of the better deals out there, and it gains access to trails like Meatball, a steep chute that funnels into a big bowl that's full of hero powder turns.

OPPOSITE: For prime backcountry, skiers strap their skis to their packs and take a worthwhile hike.

PAGES 26-27: Yurts on Red Mountain Pass in the nearby San Juan National Forest offer a chance to warm up.

many there are up there," says Jen Brill), just like in the backcountry, skiers have to hike.

One of the best hike-to trails is The Ramp, a 35-degree, open bowl that descends for 2,000 vertical feet (609.6 m). When they get off the lift, skiers can shoulder their skis or strap them to their packs, then bootpack south up the windswept ridgeline for about 20 minutes, all the while gaping at several of the San Juan's jagged, 14,000-foot (4,267.2 m) peaks. From about 12,600 feet (3,850.5 m), skiers drop into The Ramp, an east-facing slope that's almost always full of untouched snow. "There are usually only 100 skiers on the mountain," says Jen Brill. "There are so few skiers that you can almost always find powder several days after a storm."

The bottom of the trail funnels into gullies—natural half-pipes that more advanced skiers enjoy popping in and out of—before ending on a road. From here, skiers climb into a school bus for a quick ride back to the chairlift. "On the bus, you always hear people talking about their run," says Jen Brill. "They're mostly talking about how it was something they'd never experienced before."

WHERE TO STAY

Staying at the Grand Imperial Hotel is a time-trip to the late 1800s, when Silverton was a thriving mining town. The hotel was built in 1883, and, in 2015, it was restored to its original glory, using everything from the time period when the hotel was built, including authentic wallpaper and antique furniture.

TELLURIDE SKI RESORT

Must-Try Trail: See Forever

MAX ELEVATION: 13,319 feet (4,059.69 m)   **AVERAGE SNOWFALL:** 280 inches (711.2 cm)
SKIABLE TERRAIN: 2,000+ acres (809.4 ha)   **OPEN SKI SEASON:** Late November to April

Telluride is quite a sight. Situated in a box canyon in southwestern Colorado, the former gold-mining outpost is surrounded by the steep, craggy cliffs of the fluted San Juan Mountains. Thick forests of spruce, fir, aspen, and pine trees hug the north side of the town, which is lined with old red brick buildings and Victorian homes. And at the end of the canyon is Bridal Veil Falls, well-photographed twin waterfalls that thunder down a 365-foot-high (111.3 m) rock face in the summer, spring, and fall and transform into a hanging wall of blue and white ice in the winter.

That scenery can be taken in while skiing most of the trails at Telluride Ski Resort, which opened in 1972 and has become known for its precipitous inbounds, hike-to descents. To name a few, you have the rocky and narrow Gold Hill Chutes; the 1,000-vertical-foot (304.8 m) drops in Black Iron Bowl; and the nearly 50-degree slopes from the top of Palmyra Peak, at 13,319 feet (4,059.6 m), the highest point at the ski area.

But no other trail better exploits the Telluride's views than See Forever, an easy intermediate groomer that mostly wends down one of the ski area's ridgelines—a high perch that, as the name implies, allows you to see forever in every direction. From the entire length of the nearly 2.5-mile-long (4 km) trail, you'll take in the babbling waters of Bear Creek, the full scale of the box

ALTERNATIVE ROUTE

Lots of great terrain lies beyond the ski area. You can access it by flying to it aboard a Eurocopter AS350 B3e helicopter. In operation since 1982, Telluride Helitrax whisks four guests per guide into the San Juan Mountains, where groups choose from 200 acres of mellow, high-alpine bowls or steep couloirs.

OPPOSITE: Telluride receives more than 280 inches (711.2 cm) of snow a year.

PAGES 30-31: Historic Colorado Avenue in downtown Telluride has colorful shops.

canyon, and, on the clearest days, you can see all the way to the La Sal mountain range in Utah. "When my family would come to town or any friend would visit, I'd always take them to ski See Forever," says Paddy O'Connell, a ski journalist and former Telluride ski patroller. "They'd always take their phones out to take several million photos, and those would be the photos they'd show people when talking about their ski trip."

The trail begins at 12,515 feet (3,814.6 m) at the top of Revelation Bowl. A little more than 500 feet (152.4 m) down the gently rolling slope is the Alpino Vino restaurant. At 11,966 feet (3,647.2 m), it bills itself as the highest fine-dining restaurant in North America—and it's worth a visit. Outside the stone hut is a multitiered deck with teak furniture, daybeds, and sheepskin throws. Inside is furniture crafted from reclaimed wine barrels, wood beams, a fireplace, and fine wines and gourmet dishes, including homemade stuffed pastas and braised bison short ribs. "Just don't drink too much vino," says O'Connell. "Sleeping in the hut is frowned upon, and you still have several thousand feet to ski and more great views to see."

WHERE TO STAY

New Sheridan Hotel, which opened in 1891, is home to, according to locals, the best steak in town. The boutique hotel has 26 rooms, some that overlook Colorado Avenue. All were overhauled in 2008 by British designer Nina Campbell, who enhanced their Victorian decor with diamond-beveled white tiles, brass and crystal chandeliers, and damask upholstery.

MAUNA KEA VOLCANO

Must-Try Trail: Mauna Kea Volcano

MAX ELEVATION: 13,803 feet (4,207.2 m)   **AVERAGE SNOWFALL: Varies**
SKIABLE TERRAIN: Follow marked guides   **OPEN SKI SEASON: Snow dependent**

Skiing began in 1936 in one of the most unlikely of places, Mauna Kea (it means "White Mountain" in Hawaiian), a 13,803-foot (4,207.2 m) dormant volcano on the island of Hawaii. Measured from its base on the ocean floor, the volcano rises over 33,000 feet/10,058.4 m, making it the highest mountain in the world. Despite its tropical location, temperatures on the volcano can dip below freezing at the highest elevations during the winter, allowing for snowfall. Using pack mules to carry their equipment, the first skiers ascended Mauna Kea, then skied down its snowcapped peak. In the late 1960s, astronomical observatories were built at the top of Mauna Kea, and it wasn't long before Hawaii's passionate outdoor community took advantage of the access road in order to slide around on the snow. In 1970, Governor John A. Burns proclaimed the first Ski Hawaii Week, and in 1971, Olympic alpine skier Suzy Chaffee skied the mountain.

These days, it's harder to ski Mauna Kea—and for good reason. The mountain is sacred to Hawaiians, and over the years, the state has adopted strict land-use rules. Mauna Kea is considered deeply important in Hawaiian ancestry. The volcano is considered the "kupuna," or first born, of the Earth Mother and Sky Father who created the islands. Mauna Kea is described as the center of the Big Island, serving as a place of worship as well as a home to the gods. Archaeological research has found at least 263 historic properties, including

OPPOSITE: Large telescope observatories are set on the summit of Mauna Kea for astronomical research.

PAGES 34-35: You can find fresh snow and one-of-a-kind skiing on Mauna Kea, but be mindful of the volcano's sacred Hawaiian history.

141 ancient shrines, on Mauna Kea, and its summit is considered the most sacred spot of all—only accessible to the highest chiefs and priests.

Skiing and snowboarding are not permitted in areas of known archaeological sites and are confined to grounds where there's sufficient snow (Mauna Kea Rangers designate those areas through maps, temporary signs, or other directions). In addition, four-wheel-drive vehicles are required to ascend the mountain (certain sections of the road are unpaved and rocky), and when it snows, the road is closed until it's plowed, which can sometimes take an entire day. Plus, going from sea level to over 13,000 feet (3,962.4 m) can cause some people to experience altitude sickness.

Overcoming those obstacles may be worth it—as long as you are respectful of the sacred culture of the mountain. After the hour-long drive, making turns on corn snow down the barren peak of a volcano, surrounded by outcroppings of lava rocks while looking down at a sea of clouds and the Pacific Ocean, is likely one of the more surreal alpine experiences on the planet.

OFF THE SLOPES

Ski and surf on the same day? Hawaii might be the only place where that's possible without a wet suit. The nearby town of Kona has several surf spots, including Kahalu'u Bay, a good break for beginners since the waves are usually on the smaller side, and Kohanaiki Beach Park, which is known to locals as Pine Trees and is better suited for advanced surfers.

SUN VALLEY SKI RESORT

Must-Try Trail: Warm Springs

MAX ELEVATION: 9,150 feet (2,788.9 m) **AVERAGE SNOWFALL:** 220 inches (558.8 cm)
SKIABLE TERRAIN: 2,154 acres (871.7 ha) **OPEN SKI SEASON:** Late November to April

When Sun Valley was founded in 1936, the owners installed the world's first chairlifts. The ability to sit and ride up the mountain—along with staying at a luxury hotel—made the resort instantly popular, and it fast became the country's first destination ski area, attracting celebrity guests like Clark Gable, Gary Cooper, Marilyn Monroe, members of the Kennedy family, and Ernest Hemingway. But what has become the ski area's signature trail, Warm Springs, didn't have chairlift access until 30 years after the resort opened. That didn't stop skiers from sampling its terrain, many of whom were so enticed by the 35-degree steeps and the 3,200-vertical-foot (975.4 m) descent that they were willing to trek all the way to the top of 9,150-foot (2,788.9 m) Bald Mountain.

These days, a high-speed quad takes you to the top of Warm Springs, where you'll find markedly different conditions depending on the time of day. Some skiers prefer to carve down Warm Springs, which is always groomed first thing in the morning, when you can see steam billowing off Warm Springs Creek in the valley below, and you can cut turns through firm, unblemished corduroy. Others opt for the afternoon, especially in March or April, when the north-facing trail is bathed in sun, the snow is softer, and you can make sweeping turns down the 100-yard-wide (91.4 m) slope right into the base area.

OFF THE SLOPES

Sun Valley is flush with hot springs, but the three thermal baths bubbling out of Warm Springs Creek at Frenchman's Bend are particularly beloved for being raw and remote. The springs are encircled with stones, right in the river, and with temperatures around 100°F to 104°F (37.8°C to 40°C), provide the restorative heat that tired ski muscles crave.

Ski runs crisscross the mountains at Sun Valley Ski Resort, which offers 120 named trails.

SUGARLOAF MOUNTAIN

Must-Try Trail: Tote Road

MAX ELEVATION: 4,237 feet (1,291.4 m)   **AVERAGE SNOWFALL:** 200 inches (508 cm)
SKIABLE TERRAIN: 1,240 acres (501.8 ha)   **OPEN SKI SEASON:** Mid-November to May

At 3.5 miles long (5.6 km), Tote Road is one of the longer alpine trails in New England. It was cut in 1956, three years after Sugarloaf Ski Area opened, and has the look and feel of a classic New England alpine ski run: Narrow and windy, bordered by thick forest on either side, the moderately pitched trail is almost always well groomed. "It's the family run that anybody can ski—from little kids to grandparents," says Sam Bass, the former editor-in-chief of *Skiing* magazine and the grandson of one of Sugarloaf's founders. "It's like a journey, not a quick lap. If you're skiing it slowly, it can be a half-hour affair."

The trail begins at Sugarloaf's 4,237-foot (1,291.4 m) summit—the third highest peak in Maine—among rime-covered, gnarled conifers, with views of the Carrabassett Valley and Mount Bigelow, a craggy, dramatic-looking ridgeline with five distinctive peaks. As you descend, you enter the more densely forested part of the trail with birch and maple trees, skiing along gentle terrain, until, a little more than halfway down the trail, you reach Chicken Pitch, a 25-degree steep that's 500 yards long (457.2 m).

From there, the trail becomes rolly and continues to undulate all the way to the base of the mountain. "You can pop off the lips of the rolls," says Bass. "As a kid, it was a great place to practice jumps. As an adult, it's a great place to watch your kids improve their skiing."

APRÈS SKI

You can't leave Sugarloaf without trying a Bag Burger at the Bag & Kettle Restaurant, located in the ski area's village—a six-ounce beef patty served with American cheese, lettuce, tomato, curly fries, and top-secret "Bag Sauce." Pair it with a Bag Brew, which is locally brewed using provincial ingredients.

A backcountry skier takes in the views of Sugarloaf from the summit of Burnt Mountain.

WHITEFISH MOUNTAIN RESORT

Must-Try Trail: Toni Matt

MAX ELEVATION: 6,817 feet (2,078 m)   **AVERAGE SNOWFALL: 320 inches (812.8 cm)**
SKIABLE TERRAIN: 3,000 acres (1,214.1 ha)   **OPEN SKI SEASON: December to April**

Each winter, after dense fog rolls through Montana's northern Rockies, the ghosts appear. Hardly supernatural but spectacular nonetheless, these "snow ghosts," as they're known at Whitefish Mountain Resort, are alpine fir trees so thickly coated with rime ice that they bend and contort into various shapes, making them look like spooky Dr. Seuss creations. The icy specters are the result of supercooled water droplets that are carried in the fog and crystallize on the trees, and they line Whitefish's signature trail, Toni Matt.

The trail is named for a former Austrian ski champion who, in 1949, came to Whitefish—an old logging outpost with a population of about 9,000 and a strictly Montana vibe (think: dive cowboy bars and mom-and-pop hardware stores)—to run the ski school at the ski area, which had been founded in 1947 as Big Mountain. In 2007, the resort adopted Whitefish as its name, linking it to the town and community just 8 miles (12.9 km) north of the ski area. The resort now boasts 105 marked trails across 3,000 skiable acres (1,214.1 ha), half of which are considered difficult terrain.

To ski the Toni Matt trail, you ride the Big Mountain Express chairlift from the ski area's base to the top of the 6,817-foot (2,078 m) mountain. Due to its expansive views, Montana is known as Big Sky country, and the sights from here live up to the state's reputation. To the north and east is Glacier National

OPPOSITE: Ice-covered rock ledges border the turn into the East Rim at Whitefish Mountain Resort.

PAGES 42-43: During a bluebird day, ski lifts make their way past snow-buried trees.

Park, more than a million acres of mountains, lakes, and dense wilderness. And on very clear days, you can see the Canadian Rockies, some 80 miles (128.7 km) to the north. Looking south are views of Flathead Valley, including Flathead Lake, which, at almost 200 square miles (321 sq km), is the largest natural freshwater lake west of the Mississippi River in the lower 48 states.

On certain days, you might also see an eerie natural phenomenon other than snow ghosts: When the valley is filled with fog, an optical illusion makes it look as though the grim reaper has swung a giant scythe and chopped off the tops of the surrounding peaks.

The trail itself, which snakes a mile and a half (2.4 km) back down to the ski area's base village, is wide, gentle, and always groomed, making it ideal for family ski outings. Nevertheless, on cold mornings when the snow is firm, expert skiers can easily hit 30 miles per hour (48.2 km/h) on the rolling terrain. Others might prefer to duck off the groomed trail into the gladed trees, a good opportunity to ski powder stashes among the snow ghosts.

APRÈS SKI

The Bierstube, known to locals as "The 'Stube," is a German-style beer hall with Montana flair: long communal high-tops fill the timber-frame bar and western saddles hang from the rafters. At the base of the mountain, this oldest watering hole at the ski area serves local pilsners and lagers along with burgers and fries.

MOUNT BACHELOR

Must-Try Trail: Cirque Bowl

MAX ELEVATION: 9,065 feet (2,763 m)   **AVERAGE SNOWFALL: 462 inches (1,173.5 cm)**
SKIABLE TERRAIN: 4,323 acres (1,749.5 ha)   **OPEN SKI SEASON: November to May**

Visitors to Mount Bachelor, a 9,065-foot-high (2,763 m) stratovolcano located in Central Oregon's Cascade Range, are offered a truly unique experience: the ability to ski or snowboard directly into the crater of a dormant volcano. To do that, you ride the Summit chairlift, which climbs nearly to the top of the mountain, then hike for five minutes to the peak. "The views are the first thing that get you," says Matthias Giraud, a professional skier who calls Mount Bachelor his home mountain. "From the top, you can see three very different types of topography."

The jagged Cascades run north and south, from southern British Columbia, through Washington and Oregon, and into Northern California. On very clear days, you can see as far as California's Mount Shasta to the south and Washington's Mount Baker to the north. To the west are expansive swaths of dense evergreen forest interrupted only by frozen lakes. And looking east are high desert views.

Dropping into Cirque Bowl can be spicy. Skiers who are after Mount Bachelor's steepest shot can descend straight off the top of the peak, through 50-degree, 200-vertical-foot (61 m) lines in between rime-covered rock pinnacles. Those who prefer an easier entry can simply ski under the chairlift and traverse into the wide-open, treeless, 35-degree bowl, making big, sweeping turns through snow-covered lava fields for 800 vertical feet (243.8 m).

OFF THE SLOPES

Mount Bachelor gets hammered with an average of 462 inches (1,173.5 cm) of snow every year. But 22 miles (35.4 km) away, in Bend, the winter climate is usually mild, and mountain biking on some of the town's 500 miles (804.7 km) of trails, rock climbing at Smith Rock State Park, and golfing are almost always post-ski options.

Sweeping Mount Bachelor offers 121 named trails to skiers and boarders.

TIMBERLINE LODGE

Must-Try Trail: Willis

MAX ELEVATION: 11,249 feet (3,428.7 m)   **AVERAGE SNOWFALL: 560 inches (1,422.4 cm)**
SKIABLE TERRAIN: 1,415 acres (572.6 ha)   **OPEN SKI SEASON: Year-round**

In the 1980 film *The Shining*, Jack Torrance (played by Jack Nicholson), recently hired as the winter caretaker for the fictional Overlook Hotel, laments, "All work and no play makes Jack a dull boy." Worse yet, that boredom, in part, sends him on a murderous rampage. If only Jack had owned a pair of skis. Though Stephen King's novel was based on Colorado's Stanley Hotel, many exterior scenes of the "Overlook" were shot at Timberline Lodge, and just outside the hotel are 1,415 acres (572.6 ha) of alpine trails.

The lodge, of course, is much more than a just famous movie set (though it's been used as such in five films). Built with native timber and stone between 1935 and 1938, the 55,000-square-foot (5,109.7 sq m) lodge attracts two million visitors each year, drawn to it by its fascinating architecture and detail, including hand-painted murals, detailed mosaics, hand-woven upholstery, bespoke furniture, and ornate iron and woodwork. Its beauty and history have become so iconic, the lodge was declared a National Historic Landmark in 1977.

Naturally, people also come here to ski. Opened in 1938, a year after the lodge opened, the ski area operates on the southern flank of Mount Hood, an 11,249-foot (3,428.7 m) stratovolcano in northern Oregon and the tallest mountain in the state.

These days, Timberline also has the distinction of being the only resort in North America to offer year-round, lift-accessed skiing and snowboarding.

APRÈS SKI

Timberline Lodge's Cascade Dining Room prepares food with locally harvested fruits, vegetables, meat, and fish. That includes a wild mushroom skillet with fresh eggs and chanterelles in the morning, a tuna melt made with albacore from the nearby Pacific Ocean for lunch, and venison for dinner.

OPPOSITE: A skier takes his dog on a run on the morning's fresh corduroy.

PAGES 48-49: Adjacent to Timberline Lodge, skiers and snowboarders wait for a lift at Mount Hood Meadows ski resort.

The ski area also offers 3,690 vertical feet (1,124.7 m) —more than any other resort in the Pacific Northwest of the United States. And though it receives 560 inches (1,422.4 cm) of snow each winter, Timberline is best known for its summer skiing on the Palmer Snowfield. The section of the mountain that the snowfield occupies was smoothed into a gentle, consistent slope during Mount Hood's last eruption period, between 180 and 250 years ago, making it perfect for intermediates and beginners.

That said, since 1979 when the Palmer chairlift was installed (prior to that, a portable rope tow was used on the glacier), ski racers have flocked to the snowfield to hone their skills during the off-season because, at 1,532 vertical feet (467 m), it's a good, long descent. A chunk of the professional slalom and giant slalom training takes place on Willis, which is right in the middle of the glacier.

To get to Willis, you first ride the Magic Mile chairlift—now a high-speed, detachable quad. (The original mile-long double chairlift was, at the

OFF THE SLOPES

Ski, then bike. Just opened in summer 2019, Timberline's well-manicured, mostly single-track downhill mountain bike trails (you ride the lift up with your bike) wind through the forested section of the mountain, past open fields of wildflowers and over wood bridges and rock gardens. In use now are 14 miles (22.5 km) of trails, with plans to expand.

time it was built in 1938, the longest chairlift in existence.) Then you take the Palmer lift, which drops you off at 8,450 feet (2,575.6 m). From here, you can see high desert and grasslands to the east. To the west are views of farmland, the rural towns surrounding Portland, and forests of towering fir and pine trees.

In the morning, the trail is icy and fast, perfect for race training. But by around midmorning, when the sun heats up to 60°F (15.6°C) and begins cooking the snow into mush, racers start vacating Willis, allowing recreational skiers to make soft turns down the 25- to 30-degree slope.

"Nothing beats a glossy smooth corn lap down Palmer at 10 on a May or June morning," says Jeffrey Kohnstamm, whose grandfather and uncle ran the ski area. "And warm afternoon slush laps on Palmer can be a lot of fun for skiers and boarders of all types and skill levels."

ABOVE: After a day on the slopes, warm yourself up by the fireplace in the Timberline Lodge lobby.

OPPOSITE: Timberline Lodge sits, snow covered, in Mount Hood National Forest.

DEER VALLEY RESORT

Must-Try Trail: Stein's Way

MAX ELEVATION: 9,570 feet (2,917 m)   **AVERAGE SNOWFALL:** 300 inches (762 cm)
SKIABLE TERRAIN: 2,026 acres (819.9 ha)   **OPEN SKI SEASON:** December to April

The skiing at Deer Valley, one of two ski areas located in Park City, Utah—just over 30 miles (48.3 km) from Salt Lake City—is best known for its perfectly groomed trails. "I've skied all over the world and Deer Valley has, hands down, the best grooming of any ski area anywhere," says Ted Ligety, a double Olympic gold medalist in alpine skiing who grew up in Park City. "They're able to turn the hill into a perfect carpet that's not too firm and not too soft, just the optimal texture that allows you to easily make turns."

To buff out the terrain, the ski area employs 13 grooming machines that roll over about 50 percent of the resort's 2,026 skiable acres (819.9 ha), or 65 of the 103 cut trails. It's a job that takes the seasoned staff (on average, those operating the machines have 13 years of grooming experience) 17 hours each night, from 4 p.m. to 9 a.m.

The best time to ski Deer Valley's trails is first thing in the morning, when the wales of corduroy left by the grooming machines are fresh, and you can hear the zipper sound your skis make as they cut through them. The best trail for that is Stein's Way, named after Stein Eriksen, a Norwegian Olympic champion who served as director of skiing at the resort for 35 years.

"It's a long trail with flats and pitches and it's east facing, so it gets first light," says Ligety. "And it has some of the best views: Mount Timpanogos

OPPOSITE: While it's one of the best-groomed mountains in the United States, Deer Valley still offers plenty of moguls and jumps.

PAGES 54-55: The unique funicular shuttles Deer Valley St. Regis guests from the Snow Park Residences to the Upper Resort building's amenities, including four restaurants, a wine vault, and a mountain terrace.

to the southwest and the sun shining off the Jordanelle reservoir, straight ahead, the whole way down."

One of the most scenic routes on the mountain, Stein's Way was also one of the first runs opened in Deer Valley when the ski-only resort was founded in 1981 by Edgar Stern.

Popular for intermediate skiers and even advanced beginners, the run—accessed from the top of the Sultan Express quad chairlift on Bald Mountain (elevation 9,400 feet/2,864.1 m)—drops 1,300 vertical feet (396.2 m) and is just shy of a mile (1.6 km) long.

The run begins as a double-blue before quickly entering a middle black diamond section that has a fantastic 70-degree slope. You'll exit the black to a regularly groomed cruiser, and follow the blue the rest of the way to the base of Sultan Express, or take the Sultan Connection and McHenry greens back to the epicenter of Deer Valley—the Silver Lake Lodge—for access to more of the mountain or trails back down to Deer Valley's base.

APRÈS SKI

Off the hill, Deer Valley has another reputation: it's ritzy. Skiers can best indulge slope-side with a craft cocktail or champagne, along with caviar, local cheeses and charcuterie, and smoked fish at the Montage's Après Lounge. The 35,000-square-foot (3,251.6 sq m) hotel was opened in 2010 and, with the numerous fireplaces and leather couches—among other fineries—is the picture of luxury.

SNOWBASIN RESORT

Must-Try Trail: Wildcat Bowl

MAX ELEVATION: 9,350 feet (2,849.9 m) **AVERAGE SNOWFALL: 300 inches (762 cm)**
SKIABLE TERRAIN: 3,000 acres (1,214 ha) **OPEN SKI SEASON: November to April**

Snowbasin was founded in 1940, and for the next 62 years, it operated as one of the more undervalued, underappreciated ski areas in the United States. Despite its long, steep descents, gladed tree skiing, and an average annual snowfall of 300 inches (762 cm), the resort, about 40 miles (64.4 km) north of Salt Lake City, never drew massive crowds.

That began to change in the early 2000s, when the ski area was awarded the downhill and super-G races for the 2002 Winter Olympics—and went into upgrade mode. Among the additions to the resort were three new on-mountain lodges that are considered among the nicest ski area dining facilities in the world. The Olympics also brought the demand for new trails, including the Grizzly downhill course, which Daron Rahlves, a former member of the U.S. Ski Team, calls the toughest Olympic downhill course he raced during his 12-year career. These days, the course is popular for those who want to feel what it's like to descend the 45-degree steeps of an Olympic downhill.

The best of Snowbasin's trails is one of the ski area's originals: Wildcat Bowl, a 1,086-vertical-foot-long (331 m) run with a consistent 30-degree pitch that's shaped like a half-pipe. Despite increased popularity, Snowbasin still gets lighter crowds than most other Utah ski areas, and you can often find yourself the only skier on the trail, making big sweeping turns all the way up onto the gully walls of Wildcat Bowl.

WHERE TO EAT

Head to the top of the John Paul chairlift and into the John Paul Lodge, one of the restaurants built for the 2002 Olympics. Indoor and outdoor seating provides close-up views of the cliffy chutes on Mount Ogden, at 9,570 feet (2,916.9 m) the highest peak at Snowbasin, and the menu includes everything from tomato bisque to a classic burger.

With tons of snow-covered pistes and meadows, there is plenty to delight intermediate and advanced skiers throughout Snowbasin.

REVELSTOKE MOUNTAIN RESORT

Must-Try Trail: Snow Rodeo

MAX ELEVATION: 8,058 feet (2,466 m)   **AVERAGE SNOWFALL:** 413 inches (1,049 cm)
SKIABLE TERRAIN: 3,121 acres (1,263 ha)   **OPEN SKI SEASON:** Late November to April

Revelstoke Mountain Resort, with 5,620 feet (1,712 m) of vertical descent, has the longest alpine ski trails in North America. It's also one of the world's newest ski areas, opened in 2007. That said, Mount Mackenzie, the 8,074-foot (2,461 m) peak on which the ski area operates, has been a skier's paradise for decades. Located just 3 miles (4.82 km) from the town of Revelstoke—an old mining and logging outpost deep in the hinterlands of southeast British Columbia, where the Selkirk and Monashee Mountains collide—it was part of a 500,000-acre (202,342 ha) playground for backcountry enthusiasts who'd access the steep bowls, tree skiing, and cliff drops by a trek up it, a helicopter, or a snowcat.

Revelstoke still offers heli and snowcat skiing, which practically guarantees guests access to deep, untouched powder, but the mountain's most famous thigh-burning descent, Snow Rodeo, is lift accessed and groomed. The trail, which winds from the top of the ski area's highest lift all the way to the base of the mountain, is beloved for its views—the massive, ice-covered Columbia River in the valley and snowcapped peaks on the horizon—and its wide-open, steep upper section, with all 2,600 vertical feet (792 m) of it encouraging high-speed turns. "It's aptly named," says Chris Rubens, a professional skier who lives in Revelstoke. "If you let it go, you'll go really fast and catch lots of air over blind rollers. It's a total rodeo, and all you can do is hang on."

CULTURAL IMMERSION

Though Revelstoke began as a small logging and mining town in the 1800s, it had grown into one of the more prominent communities in British Columbia by the early 1900s. At one point, it was home to an opera house as well as a large department store. Skiing has long been an important part of the culture. In 1915, the first ski jump in Canada was constructed in Revelstoke.

A heli-skier rides below a corniced peak in the Columbia Mountains of British Columbia.

WHISTLER BLACKCOMB

Must-Try Trail: Peak to Creek

MAX ELEVATION: 7,494 feet (2,284 m)   **AVERAGE SNOWFALL:** 448 inches (1,138 cm)
SKIABLE TERRAIN: 8,171 acres (3,307 ha)   **OPEN SKI SEASON:** November to May

It stands to reason that the biggest ski area in North America is home to one of the continent's longest alpine trails. With a vertical drop of almost 5,000 feet (1,524 m), Peak to Creek is a 3.7-mile-long (6 km) groomed trail that starts at the top of 7,160-foot (2,182 m) Whistler Mountain and wends along the ski area's boundary all the way to Whistler Creek at the base. It's so long, in fact, that in 2004, ski area brass commissioned local artisans to design two benches with bears carved on the uprights—placed approximately 1 mile (1.5 km) apart along the trail—so that skiers and snowboarders can stop and rest during the long descent.

Skiing the trail requires taking several chairlifts, eventually riding the Peak Express lift to the top of the mountain. Garibaldi Provincial Park, including the Black Tusk (a toothy spire that juts from the snowy peaks), as well as Wedge Mountain, dominates the skyline.

The first several thousand feet of the trail are in the high alpine, above the tree line. But as you make your way down the wide run, over mellow, rolling terrain, you'll pass through two other distinct ecosystems. The second third of the trail is made up of mountain hemlock, a slender, conic evergreen that grows just below the tree line, and your final turns are past western hemlock, a broader evergreen that grows in the temperate rainforests of Whistler's lower elevations.

APRÈS SKI

Whistler is well known for its party scene, and post-ski festivities usually begin at the Garibaldi Lift Co. Bar & Grill. Located above the Whistler gondola building, the huge space, typically packed with people sipping cocktails and beers, features a large stone fireplace and patios that look out over the village and the lower ski hills.

Skiers and snowboarders enjoy the groomed runs at Whistler Blackcomb, which has more than 200 trails to choose from.

AIGUILLE DU MIDI

Must-Try Trail: Vallée Blanche

MAX ELEVATION: 12,605 feet (3,842 m) **AVERAGE SNOWFALL: 429 inches (1,089.7 cm)**
SKIABLE TERRAIN: 10 miles (16.1 km) **OPEN SKI SEASON: December to May**

Chamonix, located in the French Alps near the borders of Switzerland and Italy, attracts a broad international crowd, most of whom descend on the town for one reason: to ski and snowboard big, exposed lines on the steep, jagged surrounding mountains. "There's a joke that you can go from having an espresso to killing yourself in three minutes," says Erin Smart, a ski guide who works in the region. "It's Disneyland for adults, where safety is not guaranteed."

That said, with the help of a guide, most intermediate skiers and snowboarders can safely navigate the Vallée Blanche (White Valley), the most famous trail in the Chamonix region (and arguably one of the most famous trails in the world). Though six other ski areas surround Chamonix, the Vallée Blanche descends nearly 10 miles (16.1 km) down Aiguille du Midi, a 12,605-foot (3,842 m) peak with several needly spires, that, though its summit is accessed by two cable cars, is not a ski area. "The trail gets skied a lot, but it's big-mountain backcountry terrain," says Smart. "There's even a sign that essentially says, 'This is not a ski area, enter at your own risk.' So you do need to be equipped with backcountry ski equipment and glacier material and know how to use it."

To reach the top of the trail, you'll ascend 9,200 feet (2,804.2 m) from the valley floor. After taking the first cable car—about a five-minute ride—through

a steep forest of pines, you'll load onto a second cable car that climbs past granite walls and hanging glaciers to the top of the mountain. The cable car docks inside a cave carved into Aiguille du Midi, and from there, you'll head through a rock tunnel, over a bridge, and into another tunnel, where you'll strap your skis to your pack, attach crampons to your boots, and get your ice axe ready.

"You have to walk about 300 feet [91.4 m] down a narrow, icy ridge," says Smart. "This is usually the most exciting part of the day." It's also one of the most beautiful vantage points. To the left of the ridge you can see the town of Chamonix. To the right are the enormous glaciers covering the Vallée Blanche, as well as a close-up view of Mont Blanc, at 15,774 feet (4,807.9 m) the highest mountain in the Alps. And to the south and north, respectively, are the blue-ice-covered peaks of Switzerland and Italy.

"Once you finish making your way across the ridge and put your skis on, it's pretty easy skiing," says Smart. The classic trail down the Glacier du

WHERE TO STAY

There are some great hotels in the middle of Chamonix and you're steps from the party, but it's noisy. To get a good night's sleep and the most out of your ski day, stay at Hotel Le Morgane, a boutique hotel with comfortable, modern rooms and a spa that's close to the Aiguille du Midi cable car and within walking distance of town.

Géant follows gentle slopes past giant granite pinnacles—fang-like formations that seem to be growing right out of the snow—seracs, and around a maze of crevasses.

The two- to three-hour tour can be broken up with lunch at Refuge de Requin (*requin* means shark in French, and the hut is named after the fin-shaped rock that towers above it). The small stone construction at 8,254 feet (2,515.8 m) serves classically French meat and cheese dishes.

After your lunch break—and the chance to rest your legs—ski the rest of the way down and exit the Mer de Glace (sea of ice) glacier via a staircase, which takes you to a gondola, which in turn takes you to a train station. Upon exiting the train back in Chamonix, you're steps from Elevation 1904, a small but inviting bar with outdoor seating. "It's where most people après," says Smart. "It's a constant party."

LAGAZUOI MOUNTAINS

Must-Try Trail: Armentarola

MAX ELEVATION: 9,301 feet (2,834.9 m) **AVERAGE SNOWFALL:** 86 inches (218.4 cm)
SKIABLE TERRAIN: 5.3 miles (8.5 km) **OPEN SKI SEASON:** January to May

Clustered together among the limestone columns, sheer cliff walls, and toothy ridgelines of northern Italy's Dolomite Mountains are 12 ski areas that offer a combined total of 745 miles (1,199 km) of groomed runs—more terrain than most people can cover in a lifetime. But one trail that every visitor to the region must experience is Armentarola, an approximately 4.6-mile-long (7.4 km) descent that many consider to be the most famous trail in the region and as much a scenic, cultural, and historical tour as it is a ski run. "It's like being at a theater, where the magic and the wonder of the Dolomites flow in front of you," says Stefano Illing, a veteran of the ski industry who lives in the region. "The open panorama of the valley gives you a sense of wonder and of discovery that is unique."

Armentarola starts near the top of Lagazuoi, a 9,301-foot-high (2,834.9 m) mountain that rises up over the town of Cortina d'Ampezzo, a classic alpine village with cobblestone streets that hosted the 1956 Winter Olympics and will cohost (with Milan) the 2026 Games. "Cortina is dolce vita," says Illing. "The sweet life. Lots of beautiful hotels and restaurants with some of the best local wine in Italy."

Getting to the trail involves an almost 12-mile (19.3 m) drive through hairpins and switchbacks along the Great Dolomites Road, followed by a three-minute ride to the Lagazuoi summit aboard a cable car. Upon exiting

APRÈS SKI

Cortina mostly eschews the raucous party scene in favor of sophisticated wine bars, including Baita Fraina, which serves more than 550 Italian and international wines, and Villa Sandi-Bottega del Vino, which is known for its Aperol spritz.

OPPOSITE: Weather-protected chairlifts offer comfort while still allowing skiers to take in the snowy Dolomites on their ride to the peak.

PAGES 70-71: The main street, Corso Italia, in the center of Cortina d'Ampezzo offers a number of shops and restaurants.

the cable car, you'll find the Rifugio Lagazuoi. Built between 1964 and 1965, it's the highest and largest mountain hut in the region, complete with dormitory-style bedrooms, communal bathrooms, and a Finnish sauna. From its huge terrace, you can look out over the alpine pastures and jagged peaks of the Natural Park of the Ampezzo Dolomites, including views of Marmolada, a glaciated mountain that, at nearly 11,000 feet (3,352.8 m), is the highest peak in the range.

Almost as soon as you start descending the Armentarola, you need to stop and check out Feldwache 4, a World War I–era emplacement carved into a rock wall, just beyond the terminus of the cable car. Austro-Hungarian soldiers built the emplacement to defend the Lagazuoi saddle, and inside is a reproduction Schwarzlose machine gun.

History lesson complete, continue skiing or snowboarding down a steep, north-facing pitch that becomes progressively mellower. "Here, you ski in front of some beautiful rocky walls that have the incredible yellowish-orange color of the Dolomites," says Illing. "It gets even more charming if

WHERE TO STAY

Cortina has grand and rustic hotels, bed and breakfasts, chalets, and huts—and it also has crash pads like Rosapetra, which can best be described as mountain chic. Bathed in softwood and stone, the hotel has a modern vibe and amenities such as an indoor heated pool, sauna, various spa treatments, and a restaurant that serves a chocolate and meringue dessert constructed to look like the Dolomites.

you ski it in the afternoon. The setting sun gives the mountains a reddish glow." The trail meanders through a pine forest before reaching the Rifugio Scotoni, a stone hut with wooden shutters that looks as though it was ripped from the pages of a Grimm Brothers' fairy tale. Inside, the hut serves 400 different wines as well as homemade speck and goulash, but it is best known for its barbeque, particularly its Florentine steaks.

Fill up too much, however, and you're in trouble. The trail continues a few more miles through a wide gorge with ice-covered rock walls, where it's not uncommon to see ice climbers scaling the frozen pitches. Once you do make it to the bottom, you'll need a way back to the lifts, and your mode of transportation is unusual. "You hang onto a rope behind a horse-drawn sleigh and it pulls you along a very flat section of trail back to the lift," says Illing. "It's a special way to end a special trail."

NARVIKFJELLET SKI RESORT

Must-Try Trail: Andrebakken to Forstebakken

MAX ELEVATION: 3,290 feet (1,003 m)   **AVERAGE SNOWFALL: 94 inches (238.8 cm)**
SKIABLE TERRAIN: 6.2 miles (10 km)   **OPEN SKI SEASON: December to June**

Skiing or snowboarding down Andrebakken and Forstebakken, a linkup of two trails at Narvikfjellet, a Norwegian ski area that's deep inside the Arctic Circle, allows you the opportunity to experience two astronomical phenomena. Both trails are illuminated, and if you hit them between November and March, you have a chance of descending while looking out at the aurora borealis, green incandescent lights that shimmer in the sky. Ski the trails in June—the cold weather here allows the mountain to hold snow into the summer—and you can ski late into the evening under the midnight sun, when the sun never sets in this part of the world.

Of course, skiing or riding down Andrebakken and Forstebakken during the day in March or April (when the Arctic begins emerging from the darkness of winter) isn't bad either. The two trails are always groomed and have an average pitch of 30 degrees, steep enough to attract international ski racing events (Narvikfjellet Ski Area is hoping to hold World Cup ski races in 2027). And the daytime views are special. The mountain, which is the highest ski area in northern Scandinavia at a max elevation of 3,290 feet (1,003 m), is almost entirely surrounded by fjords, and as you cruise down the two trails— some 1,300 vertical feet (396 m) of descent—you'll look out at the red brick buildings and quaint seashore homes in the municipality of Narvik as well as shipping freighters cruising along the dark blue water.

CULTURAL IMMERSION

Sami are indigenous people in northern Norway, and many still live in the region. Traditionally, Sami were fishers, trappers, and reindeer herders, and it's still possible to see groups of native Norwegians herding reindeer in the area today. While visiting Narvik, you can sample traditional Sami food, such as sautéed or smoked reindeer served with flatbread.

The aurora borealis, as seen from the mountain, dances over the town of Narvik in Norway.

MUTNOVSKY VOLCANO

Must-Try Trail: Mutnovsky Crater

MAX ELEVATION: 7,618-foot (2,322 m)   AVERAGE SNOWFALL: 103 inches (261.6 cm)
SKIABLE TERRAIN: Backcountry   OPEN SKI SEASON: March to June

The Kamchatka Peninsula, located in the northeastern corner of Russia, is a wild frontier. Included on UNESCO's World Heritage List due to its beauty and biodiversity, the untamed wilderness is home to giant sea eagles, wolves, and all six species of Pacific salmon run, turning pristine rivers red and feeding the densest population of brown bears in the world. Separated from Alaska's Aleutian Islands by the narrow Bering Strait, Kamchatka sits on the Ring of Fire, thousands of acres of grinding tectonic plates and one of the highest concentrations of active volcanoes on Earth. Some 20 to 30 of Kamchatka's approximately 200 volcanoes still shudder with seismic activity, and at least two volcanoes on the peninsula erupt each year.

Those volcanoes, including 15,584-foot (4,750 m) Klyuchevskaya Sopka, also stall storms and accumulate huge amounts of snow, making their flanks perfect slopes for intrepid skiers and snowboarders who are willing to make the long journey to Kamchatka—and ready to rough it when they get there. Closed to the public during Soviet rule due to its military importance, Kamchatka remains sparsely populated and underdeveloped. The majority of its fewer than 400,000 residents live in the capital of Petropavlovsk, 4,000 miles (6,437.4 km) from Moscow and accessible only by plane or boat.

To get to one of the more popular ski and snowboard locales, Camp Rodnikovaya, near the southern tip of the peninsula, can be a four-day trip from

OPPOSITE: Snowboarders get ready for their descent at the Gora Moroznaya Ski Resort.

PAGE 78-79: The Kamchatka Peninsula offers a one-of-a-kind winter landscape: Gas, steam, and ashes plume from the crater of the active Avacha volcano, which is covered in snow.

the United States. While there, you'll stay in converted shipping containers that are sparsely furnished with necessities, bathe in thermal pools, eat salmon and venison, and, if you're so inclined, drink vodka (lots and lots of vodka). From the camp, you have access to thousands of acres of ski descents, but the most impressive run takes you past hissing fumaroles, bubbling mud pots, and a glacial lake, down the crater of Mutnovsky, a 7,618-foot (2,322 m) active volcano that last erupted in 2000.

To get there takes an act of courage. Accessing these peaks is easiest aboard a former military Mi-8, a twin-turbine helicopter that's not well known for its safety record. Risk it, though, and the payoff is huge. "Skiing cold, knee-deep powder into the crater of a steaming volcano is so far beyond the realm of what I thought was possible," says Kyle Smaine, a professional skier who visited Kamchatka in 2018. "It's so unique that I would never think to add it to my bucket list of ski descents because I couldn't have even imagined it was possible."

CULTURAL IMMERSION

Due to its proximity to the United States, Kamchatka was an important military zone during the Cold War. North of the Mutnovsky Volcano is Bechevinka, which was a secret submarine base during that era. Tucked into a beautiful bay, remnants of the base still exist, including dilapidated old apartment buildings and rusted submarines and ships floating in the bay. You can still visit the ghost town today.

GLENCOE MOUNTAIN RESORT

Must-Try Trail: The Flypaper

MAX ELEVATION: 3,635 feet (1,070 m)   **AVERAGE SNOWFALL:** 118.1 to 177.1 inches (300-450 cm)
SKIABLE TERRAIN: 21.1 miles (34 km)   **OPEN SKI SEASON:** Mid-December to early May

When the last ice age shaped the ancient volcanoes of the Scottish Highlands into 3,000- to 4,000-foot (9,14.4-1,219.2 m) peaks, it left ideal skiing terrain: steep, rock-walled gullies, flowing ridgelines, and open bowls. In the 1920s, Scottish skiers began exploring the peaks. But it wasn't until 1956 that a group of skiers known as the Wee Crowd opened the country's first ski resort, Glencoe Mountain Resort, built on Meall A'Bhuiridh, a 3,635-foot (1,108 m) mountain in Scotland's southwest Highlands. "Building Glencoe was a community effort," says Kenny Biggin, the author of two guidebooks to skiing in Scotland. "Guys working in the shipyards in Glasgow did the welding to construct the lifts."

The ski area has several small log cabin–style day lodges, eight lifts, and 20 trails, including the Flypaper, considered the best inbounds trail in Scotland. "It's always been one that people talk about," says Biggin, "because it's steep and feels off-piste, it can act as a gateway drug for the wild mountains that lie beyond the ski hill."

To get to the Flypaper, you take the Rannoch Button or Main Basin tow to the top of the mountain. The approximately 40-degree trail descends 748 vertical feet (228 m) and benefits from wind loading, making knee-deep turns a possibility. "It's a short run," says Biggin, "but on the right day, it can be as good as anywhere in the world."

WHERE TO STAY

The Kingshouse Hotel, just a five-minute drive from the ski area, sits right on the River Etive, where red deer graze and there are views of the Highlands outside your window. The hotel, which has been greeting travelers since the 1750s, underwent major renovations in 2017 and 2018 with a modern, cozy design.

An off-piste skier takes a jump on a descent down Glencoe Mountain.

MARIBOR POHORJE SKI RESORT

Must-Try Trail: Miranova Proga and Slalom Course

MAX ELEVATION: 4,345 feet (1,327.1 m)   **AVERAGE SNOWFALL: 25 inches (63.5 cm)**
SKIABLE TERRAIN: 617.8 acres (250 ha)   **OPEN SKI SEASON: December to March**

Skiing or snowboarding down Maribor Pohorje Ski Resort's Miranova Proga and Slalom Course trails at night is an unparalleled experience. The entire 2-mile-long (3.2 km) linkup is illuminated, making it one of the longest lighted strips of skiable terrain in Europe. While plenty of ski trails overlook quaint alpine villages and towns, the view from the two trails is of the hundreds of thousands of twinkling lights of Maribor, the second largest city in Slovenia (population: 96,000). "The city is lit up like a Christmas tree with red, yellow, and green lights from the houses, apartments, from the tops of the churches in the city center, the Maribor Castle, and the soccer arena," says Melanja Korošec, the brand director for Elan, a ski manufacturer that was founded in what was then Yugoslavia in 1945. "I've skied the trails hundreds of times at night, and that view never gets old."

Cruising down the trails during the day can also offer an otherworldly experience. Maribor Pohorje's first chairlift was installed in 1951, but for many years prior to that, city dwellers would trek to the top of the 4,354-foot (1,327.1 m) mountain to enjoy the skiing and escape the fog in the valley below. Skiing in the sun, above the clouds, is still popular at the ski area, and photos taken from the piste of the city engulfed in fog is a trendy shot for amateur photographers. "On those days, Instagram gets flooded in pictures from 'above the clouds,'" says Korošec.

OPPOSITE: The Maribor ski area boasts more than 26 miles (41.8 km) of trails, including 8 miles (13 km) for intermediates and 3 miles (5 km) for experts.

PAGES 84-85: Maribor's city center is beloved by après-ski enthusiasts, with a number of pubs, night-clubs, and discos on offer.

Though your perspective will change dramatically depending on whether you ski Miranova Proga and Slalom Course during the day or at night, the trails' conditions, thanks to state-of-the-art grooming machines and snowmaking, are remarkably consistent. The rolling terrain, which twists and turns over flat sections and pitches as steep as 52 degrees, is so well maintained, in part, because it hosts the Golden Fox, an annual women's World Cup ski race that began in 1964 (winners have included Mikaela Shiffrin and Lindsey Vonn). "The race is really what the ski area is most famous for," says Korošec. "It draws over 10,000 spectators and is one of the most watched races on the women's tour."

Whether you race down the trail or take your time, stopping at the bottom for a drink or a bite to eat at the Koča Luka is a must. The wood hut serves local sausages and beer, and the large patio faces the slopes. "On a sunny warm day, this is the place to hang out and get a tan," says Korošec. "After an evening of night skiing, it's a great place to grab a drink, hang out with friends, and watch skiers come down under the lights."

WHERE TO STAY

Hotel Habakuk, at the base of the ski area, has unobstructed views of the slopes and surrounding forest; a wellness center and spa with squash courts, a swimming pool, and several saunas; and a restaurant that serves locally harvested meats, fish, and vegetables.

DIAVOLEZZA-LAGALB SKI AREA

Must-Try Trail: Glacier Run

MAX ELEVATION: 9,770 feet (2,978 m)   **AVERAGE SNOWFALL:** 150 inches (380 cm)
SKIABLE TERRAIN: 21.7 miles (35 km)   **OPEN SKI SEASON:** Mid-October to mid-November; December to May

At the beginning of *A View to a Kill* (1985), James Bond digs around in the snow in search of a microchip. Once he finds it, he begins skiing down a glacier, through crevasses and over steep faces of corn snow, past ice flows and dramatic, jagged mountain peaks, and skims across a glacial pond, all the while being fired on by the bad guys. The scene was shot in the mountains around Saint Moritz, Switzerland, and 007's visit continued a long tradition of Brits spending time in the small Alpine town.

In September 1864, a local hotelier made a bet with a group of guests from Great Britain, who were visiting to cool off in the fresh mountain air and soak in the nearby thermal hot springs—known then (and now) for their therapeutic healing powers. He told them to come back in the winter and promised snow, sunny skies, and temperatures so warm that they could relax on the terrace without wearing a jacket. If he was wrong, their hotel stay would be comped.

The following December, the British visitors crossed the Julier Pass, arriving to find the bright sunshine they'd been promised (Saint Moritz averages 322 sunny days per year). The Brits, along with well-heeled tourists from the rest of Europe, kept coming, and by the early 1900s, Saint Moritz had become a popular winter destination.

OFF THE SLOPES

Since the Bronze Age, people have traveled to Saint Moritz to bathe in the natural, mineral-rich hot springs, which are touted for their healing properties. Treat yourself at the Mineralbad and Spa Sameden, a five-story maze of tiled baths beautifully illuminated by chandeliers.

OPPOSITE: Professional skier Ingrid Backstrom tackles terrain in Saint Moritz.

PAGES 88-89: Skiers pause just off the lift to enjoy views of the snow-covered peaks.

These days, the town is known for its glitz: five-star hotels (the 125-year-old Badrutt's Palace has suites starting at around $4,500 per night), swanky restaurants, high-end boutiques, and summer activities that have been winterized, like polo and horse racing.

It's also, of course, known for its skiing, with several hundred miles of steep, long slopes that have hosted alpine events at two Winter Olympics and five World Championships. The resort boasts five ski areas serviced by a total 56 lifts. Along with downhill skiing, St. Moritz also offers more than 100 miles (160.9 km) of Nordic cross-country ski trails.

Those who want a James Bond–like experience (without having to dodge bullets) head to Diavolezza, one of Saint Moritz's five ski areas, and ski the Glacier Run, a 6.2-mile-long (10 km) trail where most of the ski scenes for *A View to a Kill* were shot.

The approximately 45-minute descent starts at the top of the Diavolezza ski area's highest lift, a cable car that drops you off at 9,770 feet (2,978 m),

WHERE TO STAY

Instead of riding the cable car up to the top of Diavolezza in the morning to ski the Glacier Run, you can sleep at nearly 10,000 feet (3,048 m). Berghaus Diavolezza is located near the top of the cable car and has a variety of sleeping arrangements—from bunk rooms that sleep 16 in tight quarters to individual rooms. The highlight is soaking in a hot tub that's located at the highest elevation in Europe.

ABOVE: Find cozy eating and top-of-the-line dining at the luxurious El Paradiso restaurant in Saint Moritz.

OPPOSITE: Dusk settles over glowing Saint Moritz, creating a winter fairy-tale-like scene.

providing a view of the biggest mountains in the eastern Alps, some of which rise as high as 14,000 feet (4,000 m).

From there, you'll ski down a steep section of moguls and onto the Pers Glacier—which touches the Morteratsch Glacier, the largest glacier by area in the Bernina Range—past cliffs that are coated with frozen waterfalls, and onto the Morteratsch Glacier, where you'll weave past large crevasses (the trail is marked with yellow cautionary ropes so that you don't stray off course and into the abyss) and remarkable tractor trailer–size chunks of ice, which are scattered about the glacier and clinging to the peaks above.

The trail ends at a train station, where you can board a coach (your lift ticket covers the fare) and ride back to the base of the ski area, eventually making your way back to Saint Moritz to enjoy a martini at one of the many trendy bars. Shaken, not stirred.

MATTERHORN SKI PARADISE

Must-Try Trail: Klein Matterhorn to Testa II to Ventina Ghiacciaio to Ventina Goillet to Ventina Bardoney 1

MAX ELEVATION: 12,792 feet (3,899 m) **AVERAGE SNOWFALL:** 394+ inches (1,000+ cm)
SKIABLE TERRAIN: 223.7 miles (360 km) **OPEN SKI SEASON:** Year-round

Zermatt, Switzerland, and Breuil-Cervinia, Italy, two Alpine towns separated by a rocky ridgeline, have similar histories. Around the middle of the 1860s, the small agricultural communities were transformed into alpinist base camps, starting points for mountaineers looking to conquer the Matterhorn, the 14,692-foot-high (4,478.1 m) pyramidal peak that straddles the border between Switzerland and Italy and looms over the two towns. As one of the highest, most recognizable mountains in Europe, the Matterhorn remains popular among climbers. But as the sport of skiing took hold throughout Europe, the slopes above the two villages began transforming into ski destinations.

To get between Zermatt and Breuil-Cervinia, you can drive 140 miles (225.3 km) around the mountains. Or you can spend a few hours riding gondolas, trams, and chairlifts, then ski or snowboard between the two villages—the rare ski excursion for which you should carry your passport. "There most likely isn't going to be anybody who makes you present your documents," says Kris Kuster, the managing director for North American operations of Mammut, an outdoor company based in Seon, Switzerland. "But because you're crossing the border from one country to another, it's not a bad idea to have them on you."

CULTURAL IMMERSION

There are no gasoline-powered vehicles in Zermatt. The decision to keep combustion engines out of the town was made early on, in part to cut down on pollution, which locals worried might someday obscure the views of the Matterhorn.

OPPOSITE: Ski guide Matteo Calcamuggi finds his way among the crevasses of Mont-Rose's glaciers.

PAGES 94-95: Take in epic views of the Matterhorn glacier at an outdoor resort bar.

Here's how to approach the adventure. After purchasing a ticket for Matterhorn Ski Paradise in Zermatt (on the Italian side, the interconnected resort is known as Cervinia Ski Paradise), you'll load onto Matterhorn Express 1, a gondola that starts from the edge of the Swiss town. "If you wanted, you could stay in Cervinia and ski into Zermatt," says Kuster. "But Zermatt has all the nice hotels and the good nightlife, while Cervinia has all the best food. So you're better off having some fun and a nice sleep in Zermatt, then skiing into Italy to have some of the best meals of your life."

After taking three more lifts, eventually cruising into thin air aboard Matterhorn Glacier Ride, billed as the highest gondola in the Alps, you'll arrive at the top of the ski area, a 12,792-foot-high (3,899 m) perch that allows you to see the Matterhorn, 38 other peaks above 14,000 feet (4,267.2 m), and 14 glaciers. "Because there are so many enormous peaks, it's one of the most impressive views in Europe," says Kuster.

WHERE TO STAY

Grand Hotel Zermatterhof opened in 1879 and has been considered one of the most luxurious digs in one of the poshest towns in Switzerland ever since. Naturally, you get to the hotel from the train station via a horse-drawn carriage. Naturally, the full-service spa has an indoor heated pool with a waterfall feature. Naturally, many of the rooms look directly out at the Matterhorn, often immersed in alpenglow or lit up by the moonlight.

ABOVE: **You'll find plenty of fresh, untouched snow while ski touring in Zermatt.**

OPPOSITE: **The** *Glacier Express* **sightseeing train connects two major mountain resorts: Zermatt and Saint Moritz in the central Swiss Alps.**

The views as you descend into Italy are pretty spectacular too. Often bathed in sunshine (the area averages 226 sunny days per year), the 6.5-mile (10.5 km) linkup of trails into Cervinia—Klein Matterhorn, Testa II, Ventina Ghiacciaio, Ventina Goillet, and Ventina Bardoney 1—are always groomed and moderately pitched, allowing for lazy turns or high-speed arcs. Along the way, you'll look out at glaciers pouring down the sides of needly peaks and pass five mountain hut restaurants, all of them flying Italian flags and serving espresso, local wines, and every regional delicacy that you can imagine: *valdostana* (pan-seared chicken cutlets with melted prosciutto and fontina cheese), roe deer ravioli, and cannelloni stuffed with potatoes and porcini mushrooms, among others. When you arrive in Cervinia after eating your way down the slope, you'll be excused for not wanting to do any more skiing. Fortunately, you can ride lifts all the way back to Zermatt.

CERRO CATEDRAL

Must-Try Trail: Panorámica

MAX ELEVATION: 7,152 feet (2,179.9 m)   **AVERAGE SNOWFALL:** 118.1 inches (299.7 cm)
SKIABLE TERRAIN: 2,965 acres (1,200 ha)   **OPEN SKI SEASON:** June to October

"Breathtaking." "Magical." "Like a slice of heaven." These are some of the ways that visitors to Cerro Catedral, a ski area in eastern Patagonia, describe the views from the mountain. It stands to reason: the resort is located inside Nahuel Huapi National Park, a 2-million-acre (809,371.3 ha) chunk of land with a remarkable landscape that includes rainforests, massive lakes, and the snowcapped peaks of the Andes.

Not only is Cerro Catedral one of the few ski areas in the world located inside a national park, it's also the largest ski area in South America. Named for the gothic-church-like granite spires that rise up from the top of the mountain, the resort has 75 miles (120.7 km) of trails and a plethora of chutes, bowls, and gladed trees.

But only Panorámica, named for the panoramic views the trail provides as you descend it, allows skiers and snowboarders to thoroughly behold the magnificent surroundings. Starting atop the 7,152-foot (2,179.9 m) mountain, the mellow groomed trail snakes down a prominent ridgeline on the ski area's boundary (locals call the trail El Filo, which means "the edge"). On the run, there are overlooks of several prominent peaks, including Cerro Tronador, an 11,453-foot (3,490.9 m) glaciated stratovolcano, as well as Lago Nahuel Huapi—the largest (205 square miles/530.9 sq km) and deepest (up to 1,522 feet/463.9 m deep) lake in Argentina.

APRÈS SKI

About halfway down Panorámica, you'll find Refugio Lynch, an alpine hut that serves Argentinian classics. On warm days, you can order your food, then move up to the deck, enjoy the famous views, and chow on lamb *carbonada*—a regional stew made with corn, pumpkin, and sweet potato—and sip a Malbec.

A skier finds untouched snow—and stumps for jumps—in the forest around Cerro Catedral.

NEVADOS DE CHILLÁN

Must-Try Trail: Las Tres Marias

MAX ELEVATION: 10,452.8 feet (3,186 m) **AVERAGE SNOWFALL:** 360 inches (914.4 cm)
SKIABLE TERRAIN: 1,383 acres (559.7 ha) **OPEN SKI SEASON:** June to October

N evados de Chillán, located in the Andes Mountains of central Chile, is one of the few ski areas in the world that operates on the slopes of an active volcano. As recently as 2018, an eruption shot plumes of ash into the air, coating the snow with black soot as skiers and snowboarders carved down the flanks of the mountain.

Over centuries, lava flows from the volcano have helped mold the upper mountain into a skier's and snowboarder's playground, an organic terrain park of natural half-pipes, wide-open bowls, spiny ridges, and smooth lips, all of which complement the lower mountain's moss-draped forests. "The resort feels alive with steaming fumaroles and volcanic plumes, and the landscapes are stunning in every direction," says Ingrid Backstrom, a professional skier who has hosted women's freeride camps at Chillán. "One of the most exciting moments I had there was seeing a flock of wild parrots."

The ski area operates on 1,383 acres (559.7 ha) of terrain, a little more than 50 percent of it tailored toward beginner and intermediate skiers and snowboarders. Nevertheless, elite ski racers from North America and Europe flock to Chillán during the Northern Hemisphere summer to train on famed runs like Huemul, Embudo, and Burro, a linkup of slopes with 25- to 30-degree pitches that, due to consistent winds that buff the track into a smooth

OPPOSITE: Nothing makes for a better ski day at Nevados de Chillán than fresh powder and a stunning sunset.

PAGES 102-103: A skier goes airborne off a ramp in the snowpark at Nevados de Chillán.

hardpack, tend to have perfect snow conditions for ski racing. In the 1980s, those ideal conditions led the brass at Chillán to designate Huemul as a speed skiing track, where one brave soul hit a top speed of 135.5 miles per hour (218.1 km/h), at the time, one of the fastest speeds ever recorded on a pair of skis.

It's not the only superlative Chillán boasts. The ski area has the longest (and possibly the slowest) chairlift in Chile, as well as the longest trail in South America. Descending for 8 miles (12.9 km), Las Tres Marias isn't Chillán's most difficult run, but skiing down it does provide some of the region's best views. "It's flat and windy," says Backstrom. "But the scenery is amazing."

From the top of the Mirado chairlift at almost 8,000 feet (2,438.4 m), Las Tres Marias hugs the skier's right boundary of Chillán and looks out at three overlapping volcanos—Volcán Nevado, Volcán Chillán, and Volcán Nuevo—all higher than 10,000 feet (3,048 m). The run cruises through the lunar landscape, sweeping wide before gradually carving back toward the base area through an evergreen forest.

APRÈS SKI

As famous for its thermal pools as it is for its skiing, Chillán's hot volcanic waters are filled with iron, sulfur, manganese, magnesium, and potassium and offer soothing relief to tired quads. Opt for the developed pools, and enjoy a pisco sour at the swim-up bar, or ski-tour to the adjacent Valle de Aguas Calientes, where a boiling river offers spots to soak in the wild.

SKI PORTILLO

Must-Try Trail: Lake Run

MAX ELEVATION: 10,860 feet (3,310.1 m)
SKIABLE TERRAIN: 1,235 acres (499.8 ha)
AVERAGE SNOWFALL: 201 inches (510.5 cm)
OPEN SKI SEASON: Late June to early October

There are plenty of alpine ski trails that provide views of big, glassy lakes as you make your way down them, but very few end right on the lake. Lake Run is one of them.

Lake Run is one of 35 trails at Ski Portillo, a remote ski area with a small infrastructure (there are only a couple hotels and restaurants) located in the central Andes Mountains. Well above the tree line at 10,000 feet (3,048 m), the trails are spread out over open snowfields that encircle the turquoise lake. Rocky peaks as high as 15,000 feet (4,572 m) rise above the slopes, dominating the skyline in every direction. When storms roll in here, they can become trapped among the mountains and last several days, depositing 2 to 3 feet (0.6 to 0.9 m) of snow.

When that happens, Lake Run, a 35-degree, 700-foot (213.4 m) descent, becomes a powder skier's dream: turn after turn through chest-deep snow, all the way to the shores of Laguna del Inca, the 2.5-mile-long (4 km) lake. If the lake is frozen, you can skate across it back to the chairlifts. If it's not, you can take the Inca Trail, a narrow path cut through a craggy section of mountain, where you're likely to see a few vizcachas—rodents that look like a cross between a rabbit and a squirrel. No matter how you get back to the lifts, chances are you'll have plenty of time for another run: the lifts at Ski Portillo stay open until 5 p.m., at least an hour longer than most other ski areas.

OFF THE SLOPES

The heated pool just outside the Portillo Hotel is the place to be after a long day of skiing. Here, you're likely to rub elbows with professional ski racers who come here to train during the off-season (Bode Miller and Lindsey Vonn were known to frequent the pool during their careers).

For the ultimate muscle-soother, take a dip in a heated pool at the foot of Portillo's epic slopes.

SKI ARPA

Must-Try Trail: Sacacorcho

MAX ELEVATION: 12,500 feet (3,740 m)   **AVERAGE SNOWFALL:** 200 inches (508 cm)
SKIABLE TERRAIN: 4,000+ acres (1,618.7+ ha)   **OPEN SKI SEASON:** Mid-June to mid-October

In 2006, Toni Sponar and his son Anton bought a snowcat to shuttle potential investors around 5,000 acres (2,023.4 ha) of craggy terrain above the Arpa Valley, a snowy, desolate plot of land high in the Andes Mountains. The elder Sponar had bought the property in 1980 and attempted to start a ski area there a few years later (the lone rope tow was taken out by an avalanche).

Decades later, he was hoping that by giving potential investors a taste of the skiing conditions, they'd be impressed enough to bankroll new lifts, lodges, and other infrastructure needed to start a new ski area. Then he got another idea. "They kept asking to be shuttled up again for another run," says Anton Sponar. "And so we realized that we didn't really need investors and we didn't need lifts—we had everything we needed."

In 2006, the Sponars opened Ski Arpa, a ski area that relies solely on snowcats to transport skiers and snowboarders up the mountain. To get to the ski area from Santiago (the closest city), you drive 65 miles (104.6 km) through fertile valleys that are home to vineyards and avocado farms, eventually climbing above the tree line, through a desert, past red rock and cactus, before arriving at the base of the mountain, 8,530 feet (2,600 m) above sea level. Here, you'll find two small stone warming huts with wood-burning stoves and snacks (a bigger lodge where guests can stay overnight is in the works).

OPPOSITE: Ski Arpa offers steep and challenging runs, with a vertical drop of nearly 3,000 feet (914.4 m).

PAGES 108-109: Snowcats, rather than lifts, are the mode of transportation for skiers at Ski Arpa. The cats operate in two valleys: Valle el Arpa and Valle la Honda, in the shadow of the Cerro Aconcagua mountain.

After loading into a snowcat, it's about a 30-minute ride to the top of the ski area, a 12,500-foot (3,740 m) perch with close-up views of 22,841-foot (6,962 m) Aconcagua—the highest mountain in South America—to the east and, on very clear days, the Pacific Ocean to the west. From here, you have a choice of 35 runs, but the fan favorite is Sacacorcho, which means "corkscrew" in Spanish. "We named it after the trail Corkscrew in Aspen," explains Anton Sponar. "It's similar because it's a gully-like trail located high on the mountain. It's not technically that challenging, but it's a crowd-pleaser because it has a nice, consistent pitch for 1,000 vertical feet [304.8]. People always want to go back to it."

That's particularly the case when storms blow in and deposit 2 to 3 feet (0.6-0.9 m) of snow. Powder skiing, especially in Sacacorcho, is always possible. *Arpa* means "harp" in Spanish, and the name is given to the valley because the intense winds that blow through here make the sound of the instrument. "They also blow snow from other parts of the mountain onto the ski trails," says Sponar, "so there's always powder to be found."

WHERE TO STAY

Among the vineyards and avocado groves of Los Andes, about 20 miles (32.2 km) south of Ski Arpa, is the Termas de Jahuel, a hotel and spa with thermal pools fed by natural hot springs, comfortable rooms (some with fireplaces) with views of the verdant valley, and a restaurant that serves local fish and beef.

RUSUTSU SKI RESORT

Must-Try Trail: Heavenly Trees

MAX ELEVATION: 3,261 feet (994 m)   **AVERAGE SNOWFALL: 512 inches (1,300.4 cm)**
SKIABLE TERRAIN: 523.9 acres (212 ha)   **OPEN SKI SEASON: December to March**

Skiers and snowboarders are drawn to Japan each winter for one reason: there's no other place in the world where powder turns are virtually guaranteed. Like everything else in the Land of the Rising Sun—snow monkeys bathing in hot springs, pagodas dripping with icicles, giant snow sculptures of dragons, bottomless bowls of ramen—the nonstop snowstorms feel magical, like something out of a children's book or like you're living inside a snow globe. But the phenomenon is purely meteorological.

From December to March, cold air from Siberia blows across the Sea of Japan, picking up moisture and depositing it on the country's mountains. That weather pattern is rumored to dump some 1,200 to 1,500 inches (30.5–38.1 m) of snow on parts of Japan. Throughout the country, as much as 10 feet (3.1 m) of snow clings to sloped rooftops, making them look like overfrosted gingerbread houses, and 20- to 30-foot-high (6.1-9.1 m) snowbanks line the roads.

One spot that benefits from all those storms is Rusutsu, located on the country's island of Hokkaido—the northernmost of Japan's main islands. The sprawling ski area, which consists of three peaks and 523.9 acres (212 ha) of skiable terrain, has a large hotel with several restaurants, as well as an amusement park with more than 60 attractions that operates during the

OPPOSITE: Skier Frederike van Dantzig descends among snow-covered birch trees in Rusutsu.

PAGES 112-113: Near the small town of Rausu, on Hokkaido's east end, the torii gate of a small Shinto shrine stands bright in the snowfall.

summer. Night skiing is popular at Rusutsu (floodlights illuminate 2.1 miles/3.3 km of trails), and skiing down the trails in a snowstorm, while overlooking the dark outline of a Ferris wheel, seems otherworldly, as does skiing Rusutsu's best run, the area aptly known as Heavenly Trees. (Take note: This is a name given to the area by locals; on the trail map, this section is unnamed but easily identified as the tree-filled bowl between the East No. 2 Pair lift and the East No. 2 Gondola—both serving as access points to the beloved route.)

Snow sticks to the birches here, making them look like big cotton swabs, and skiing between the well-spaced trees, through deep powder stashes in the quiet solitude of the woods, feels like floating through the clouds.

"This area is a natural playground for any ability skier," says Charlie Cohn, co-owner of Adventure-Locals, a service that organizes ski trips throughout Japan. "It's the perfect pitch for submarining through that legendary Japanese powder."

The 35-degree slope starts at the top of East Mountain (2,847.8 feet/868 m above sea level) and

APRÈS SKI

Just down the road from Rusutsu's massive hotel and carnival-like atmosphere is a tiny, unassuming hole-in-the-wall, Rodeo Drive bar. Inside the shack-like structure is enough room for about two dozen people to drink beers or, better yet, have a glass of Japanese whiskey, a spirit that connoisseurs believe is on par with scotch.

descends for some 1,000 vertical feet (304.8 m) on a V-shaped bowl in the middle of the peak. On clear days—which are rare—you can look out and see, to the northwest, Mount Yotei, a nearby volcano located inside the Shikotsu-Toya National Park, and, to the south, the Pacific Ocean.

"You can traverse as far as you want through extra well spaced trees and simply pick your line and drop in whenever you get that gut feeling telling you to do so," says Cohn. "There is plenty of fun to be had on the ground, but also countless features like small drops and shrubby trees, which are piled with snow and sort of look like mushrooms, to jump on and off."

The best part: You can ski the Heavenly Trees all day and always find fresh powder turns. Because it's usually hammering snow, old tracks fill in quickly, a wonder that skiers and snowboarders refer to as "free refills."

HAKUBA HAPPO-ONE SNOW RESORT

Must-Try Trail: Olympic Course I

MAX ELEVATION: 6,007.2 feet (1,831 m) **AVERAGE SNOWFALL:** 460.6 inches (1,170 cm)
SKIABLE TERRAIN: 544 acres (220 ha) **OPEN SKI SEASON:** Mid-November to early May

Olympic Course I is responsible for one of the most famous crashes in skiing history. In 1998, Hakuba Happo-One Snow Resort hosted the Winter Olympics' alpine ski racing events. The men's downhill course was designed by Bernard Russi, an Olympic champion from Austria, and sent skiers nuking down the 1,276-vertical-foot (388.8 m) slope at an average speed of nearly 68 miles per hour (109.4 km/h) through big sweeping turns, a corridor of trees, and some 200 feet (61 m) off three big jumps.

Sixteen seconds into the race, Austrian skier Hermann Maier went around a turn, hit a bump, and catapulted off the course, flying approximately 200 feet (61 m) in the air before landing in the fencing. It became known as *der sturz* (the fall, in German), and the photo of Maier in the air, his body horizontal to the ground, became iconic, gracing the cover of *Sports Illustrated*. (Maier was unhurt and went on to win two gold medals at those Olympics.)

There's an easy way to avoid Maier's fate: Don't ski that fast. In fact, when you're not racing down Olympic Course I, the trail is rather gentle. Always groomed and with an average pitch of 31 degrees, it's beloved for its views of the Hakuba Valley and the fluted Japanese Alps. "It's a classic top-to-bottom, on-piste run that can cap off any good day of skiing at Happo-One," says Charlie Cohn, co-owner of AdventureLocals. "And it takes you right into an iconic Japanese ski town—a mix of fine dining, quirky bars, and food trucks."

OFF THE SLOPES

With 110 active volcanoes, the Japanese have discovered the most blissful way to use all that thermal activity via *onsens*, bathing facilities fed by natural hot springs. In Hakuba, the Highland *onsen* is across the valley from Happo-One. An indoor-outdoor pool is lined with stones and looks directly at the ski area.

Skiers wind down a tree-lined trail in Hakuba Happo-One Snow Resort, which offers 544 acres (220 ha) of skiing.

NISEKO HANA-ZONO RESORT

Must-Try Trail: Strawberry Fields

MAX ELEVATION: 3,743.4 feet (1,141 m) **AVERAGE SNOWFALL:** 590.5 inches (1,499.9 cm)
SKIABLE TERRAIN: 128.5 acres (52 ha) **OPEN SKI SEASON:** December to April

Japan's north island of Hokkaido is flush with coveted powder runs, but none more famous than Strawberry Fields, a 912-foot-long (278 m), 30-degree slope that Japan's wintertime storms and favorable winds load with deep snow. How deep? "Sometimes so deep it's hard to move," says Chris Davenport, a professional skier who guides trips to Japan. "It's all avalanche controlled and safe, but I always recommend people wear a beacon because I've seen people fall and get buried just because the snow is so deep."

Strawberry Fields takes up a large, northeast-facing swath of terrain at Niseko Hanazono, a ski area that shares Mount Niseko Annupuri, a 4,291.3-foot (1,308 m) dormant volcano, with three other ski areas—Annupuri, Niseko Village, and Grand Hirafu. You can ski back and forth between all of them with the Niseko United ski pass. "It's fun to bounce among all of the ski areas throughout the day," says Davenport. "But everybody heads to Strawberry Fields first."

Get there by riding the Hanazono chairlift 1 from the base of Hanazono. From there, you can traverse along the top of Strawberry Fields until you find a line that appeals to you. "I like to go pretty far out," says Davenport. "You lose some elevation, but almost nobody goes out there, so you can usually always find fresh tracks through well-spaced birches, over little rock drops, and through drainage gullies that are like little half-pipes."

WHERE TO STAY

Zaborin is a traditional Japanese lodge with a twist of luxury. The *ryokan* (or inn) is composed of 15 villas with tatami-matted floors, private outdoor *onsens* (hot spring baths chiseled from stone), a cigar room, and candlelit outdoor foot baths, which, during the winter months, are accessed by tunnels carved through huge snow drifts.

The snow sculptures outside the Niseko train station make for the perfect photo opp.

THREDBO ALPINE VILLAGE

Must-Try Trail: Supertrail

MAX ELEVATION: 6,670 feet (2,033 m) **AVERAGE SNOWFALL:** 83 inches (210.8 cm)
SKIABLE TERRAIN: 1,200 acres (480 ha) **OPEN SKI SEASON:** June to October

Thredbo, located in southeastern Australia's Snowy Mountains—right between Melbourne and Sydney—was founded in 1956 and by the 1980s had become well known for two activities: mogul skiing and partying. By the 1990s, snowboarding had also become extremely popular at Thredbo, and the resort's trails helped several riders become international stars, including 2010 Olympics gold medalist Torah Bright.

Thredbo's iconic trail—with a vertical drop of 2,149 feet (655 m), Australia's longest run—is Supertrail, which starts atop the ski area's 6,670-foot (2,033 m) peak. The trail is best experienced first thing in the morning, for two reasons. First, it's groomed at night, so an early start gives you the opportunity to sink your edges into a fresh track. Second, you might have the chance to see a meteorological phenomenon: the rounded peaks of the Snowy Mountains poking through a dense layer of clouds that envelope the valley below.

From the top of the trail, you wind your way down through the high alpine before reaching the Eagles Nest, a rollover just above the tree line that takes you down the steepest part of Supertrail. From here, you continue to descend past snow gums—shrubby-looking eucalyptus trees—and into the ski area's base. "Supertrail isn't the most difficult trail out there," says Simon Blondel, the cofounder of Le Bent, a ski sock manufacturer. "But if you ski it top to bottom, it's the only trail in Australia that can give you a leg burn."

APRÈS SKI

Visitors to Thredbo love to party. There are dozens of bars but only one night-club. Really more of a late night party spot than an establishment you'd hit right after skiing, Keller Bar is a rowdy scene where patrons pack in tightly, slosh drinks around, and dance on a sticky floor to music spun by local DJs.

Olympian skier and Thredbo local Jono Brauer skis the Bluff. Thredbo is known for having Australia's longest runs and steepest vertical terrain.

CRAIGIEBURN VALLEY SKI AREA

Must-Try Trail: Hamilton Face

MAX ELEVATION: 6,305 feet (1,922 m) **AVERAGE SNOWFALL:** 350 inches (889 cm)
SKIABLE TERRAIN: 350 acres (141.6 ha) **OPEN SKI SEASON:** July to September

The proprietors of Craigieburn Valley Ski Area are as proud of what they do have—350 acres (141.6 ha) of steep chutes and open powder faces—as what they don't have: "You will not find any chairlifts, gondolas, grooming, snowmaking, golf courses, day spas, or fine dining here," reads Craigieburn's website.

Located between Springfield and Arthur's Pass on South Island, Craigieburn is operated by a nonprofit ski club, which maintains a stripped-down infrastructure and laid-back atmosphere. A no-frills cinder block and corrugated metal hut serves as the day lodge; on the trail map, expert runs are labeled "tricky stuff"; and the only uphill conveyances are three rope tows, which only take you so far. Accessing much of the terrain requires hiking.

A 20-minute trek takes you to the top of 6,305-foot-high (1,922 m) Hamilton Peak, the highest point at the ski area. Atop the mountain you have uninterrupted views of the Southern Alps. The descent, 1,722 vertical feet (524.9 m) down Hamilton Face, is the longest run at the ski area. The moderately steep trail is wide open and often brimming with deep snow.

"You're above tree line looking out at a lunar-like landscape that's full of powder and there's hardly anybody else out skiing," says Andy Bardon, a contributing *National Geographic* photographer. "I spent a week skiing at Craigieburn and never crossed another track the whole time."

OFF THE SLOPES

Arthur's Pass is a multisport paradise. After skiing you can head down the road to Castle Hill and climb acres of giant limestone rocks that contain thousands of boulder problems. Or you can navigate through Cave Stream, an underground passage that snakes through a limestone cavern for almost a quarter mile.

A father and son ski duo plan their descent down the 210 Chute, so named because it is only 210 centimeters (82.7 in) wide.

MOUNT HUTT SKI AREA

Must-Try Trail: Jan's Face to Muesli Bowl

MAX ELEVATION: 7,185 feet (2,190 m)   **AVERAGE SNOWFALL: 157 inches (398.8 cm)**
SKIABLE TERRAIN: 901.9 acres (365 ha)   **OPEN SKI SEASON: June to October**

Mount Hutt, located on the eastern rim of New Zealand's Southern Alps, was opened in 1973 by locals, for locals, and despite the fact that it now caters to a broad international crowd, it is still mostly regional. "Mount Hutt has a very strong local identity," says Mike Unger, who spends his winters in Methven, the town at the base of the mountain and in 2019 skied approximately 1.1 million vertical meters at Mount Hutt, a record at the ski area.

Because of the mostly regional crowd, skier numbers can be light—except on powder days. A good dump at Mount Hutt consists of 1 to 2 feet (0.3-0.6 m) of snow, and, despite the larger crowds, you can still find fresh turns. Many of Unger's vertical miles were logged on Jan's Face and Muesli Bowl, two trails at the very edge of the ski area's boundary that skiers often overlook.

To get to the trails, skiers and snowboarders ride a six-person lift to the summit of the 7,185-foot (2,190 m) mountain—views from here stretch across the Canterbury Plains, a patchwork quilt of grasslands and farmlands, all the way to the Pacific Ocean—before traversing down a ridgeline. "People don't go out that far," says Unger. "They get excited and drop in early." As such, Unger says, you can usually make four runs down the two trails, which have 35- to 40-degree pitches and combine for 1,500 vertical feet (457.2 m) of descent, and still find stashes of untouched snow on each run.

OFF THE SLOPES

Located atop Mount Hutt is the highest hot tub in New Zealand. There's a nearby changing room where you can strip off your ski gear, throw on your swimsuit, and enjoy a soak while watching skiers making turns down the mountain. The only downside: once you've finished, you have to get dressed and ski back down.

A trail post marks the way to some of Mount Hutt's most difficult named terrain.

Sunlight illuminates Haines Pass in Alaska's Chilkat Range, home to some of the world's best heli-skiing.

ADVANCED

TORDRILLO MOUNTAINS, ALASKA, UNITED STATES

MOUNT SPURR

Must-Try Trail: 6500

MAX ELEVATION: 11,070 feet (3,374.1 m)   **AVERAGE SNOWFALL:** 600 to 800 inches (1,524-2,032 cm)
SKIABLE TERRAIN: 1.2 million acres (485,622.8 ha)   **OPEN SKI SEASON:** February to July

Heli-skiing was born in the Canadian Rockies, but Alaska made it famous. For some 40 years, ski movies have featured men and women flying in helicopters to 5,000-vertical-foot (1,524 m) couloirs, spines, and massive powder bowls—terrain that only Alaska has and that only a helicopter can access. The most famous of those descents have names like Sphinx, Meteorite, and Pontoon—runs so steep that the snow sloughs off them as skiers and snowboarders descend, sometimes taking them out at the ankles and sending them on a long, violent tumble.

But not all Alaskan heli-skiing descents are treacherous. Over the past few decades, several operations have sprung up that cater to intermediate and advanced skiers. One of the more coveted heli-skiing destinations for well-heeled weekend warriors is Tordrillo Mountain Lodge (TML), which was founded in 2004 by Mike Overcast, a long-time Alaskan ski guide, and Tommy Moe, a former Olympic champion.

The small campus of luxury cabins is situated deep in the Alaskan backcountry, 60 miles (96.6 km) northwest of Anchorage, and is accessible only via a single-engine plane that takes off from Anchorage and lands 40 minutes later on a frozen lake, just steps from the main lodge.

Part of what makes heli-skiing special is the accommodations, and TML's lodging is among the industry's more opulent options. There are hot tubs,

ALTERNATIVE ROUTE

You can still ski 6500 when it is covered in corn snow. In June and July, TML offers guests an experience called Kings and Corn, which involves corn skiing on the Tordrillos' sun-cooked faces in the morning, followed by king salmon fishing in the afternoon.

OPPOSITE: Alaska's Tordrillo Mountains are mostly untapped wilderness with nearly 1 million acres (404,685.6 ha) to explore.

PAGES 130-131: A bright light in the wilderness of Alaska, Tordrillo Mountain Lodge glows in the snowscape.

a lounge with a wood-burning stove and leather couches, a bar with neon lighting and top-shelf liquor, a 500-bottle wine cellar, professional massage services, daily yoga, a lakeside copper hot tub and cedar sauna, the fastest Internet connection in all of Alaska (stock trades can still be completed in milliseconds), and five-course meals every night, including sushi that's served on giant powder skis. Guests can stay in the Main Lodge, one of two private cabins adjacent to the main facility, the four-bedroom Judd Lake Lodge, or the lakeside retreats by Moose Hall. If it weren't for the fact that TML has access to skiing and snowboarding on 1.2 million acres (485,622.8 ha) of the nearby 11,000-foot (3,352.8 m) peaks, you wouldn't want to leave the lodge at all.

To access that terrain, you load onto an A-Star helicopter and take a short flight into the Tordrillo Mountains, a 60-mile-long (96.6 km) volcanic range that overlooks giant columns of blue ice and moraines on surrounding glaciers, as well as boats bobbing on the Cook Inlet. In a single day,

OFF THE SLOPES

All winter, a hole cut in the ice in Judd Lake, just outside the main lodge, serves as a polar plunge. Optimal plunging goes like this: After cooking in the nearby sauna for 10 minutes, you run about 50 yards down to the lake, jump in, then head back to the sauna. Rumor has it that surfing great Laird Hamilton, who has visited TML to snowboard, stayed submerged in the frozen waters for four minutes.

ABOVE: Soak sore muscles after a day on the mountain in Tordrillo Mountain Lodge's hot tub at Moose Hall.

OPPOSITE: With acres and acres to cover, you'll find plenty of opportunity to carve fresh tracks in the Alaska mountain range.

skiers and snowboarders can take around eight runs, logging an incredible 30,000 vertical feet (9,144 m) of descent.

Among the best of those runs is 6500, which gets its name because the trail starts 6,500 feet (1,981.2 m) up the eastern flank of Mount Spurr—about halfway up the peak. "You have some of the best views from that trail," says Moe.

Descending a total of 4,000 vertical feet (1,219.2 m) through the Capps Glacier, a wavy expanse of snow dunes, you snake through crevasses and into an open bowl of mellow, 30-degree slope that's often filled with deep powder. From there, you ski into a narrow couloir that's 35 degrees steep.

"It kind of feels like you're in a tunnel," says Moe. "Then you exit onto a big open area where you're skiing past seracs and looking back on the hanging ice cliffs on Mount Spurr. I've had some of my best runs down 6500. It's the trail guests usually ask to go ski again."

SQUAW VALLEY ALPINE MEADOWS

Must-Try Trail: Chute 75

MAX ELEVATION: 9,050 feet (2,758.4 m) **AVERAGE SNOWFALL:** 450 inches (1,143 cm)
SKIABLE TERRAIN: 4,000 acres (1,618.7 ha) **OPEN SKI SEASON:** November to May

Squaw Valley, which overlooks Lake Tahoe in Northern California, is a ski area that feels as though it has been flipped upside down. Unlike most other resorts, Squaw's beginner terrain is found near the 9,050-foot (2,758.4 m) peak, while its expert trails—steep, intimidating lines—are front and center, the first thing you see as you walk through the busy, European-style village.

The most challenging terrain is found off the KT-22 chairlift, 2,000 vertical feet (609.6 m) of cliff bands, chutes, open bowls, and glades accessed by the chairlift. "Squaw is a lazy person's mountain because all the chairlifts take you to everything you want to ski," says Connery Lundin, a professional skier who calls Squaw home. "You don't need to traverse or hike to anything."

Chute 75, one of the truly iconic trails in the United States, is just a short ski from the top of the KT-22 lift. The 40-degree, nearly 1,000-vertical-foot-long (304.8 m) chute skis well when it's filled with moguls or wind-loaded with chalky snow, but making first turns down it on a powder day is a prize most serious skiers covet. To do that takes some effort. "On a powder day, skiers will get up at 5 a.m., put a breakfast burrito in their pockets, and wait in line for hours to get the first chair," says Lundin. "If you're lucky enough to be the first one in the chute, you'll have perfect north-facing powder turns, the kind that people pay big money to fly in a helicopter to get to."

APRÈS SKI

Wildflour Baking Company, located in the village, is a shrine to local athletes who've grown up skiing at Squaw. Photos of Olympic champions Julia Mancuso and Jonny Moseley, to name a few, adorn the walls, and the small shop smells of freshly baked cookies, including pumpkin walnut chocolate chip, toffee nut, and peanut butter.

Skiers stand on a ridge to catch their breath before a descent into Squaw Valley's terrain.

MAMMOTH MOUNTAIN SKI AREA

Must-Try Trail: Dave's Run

MAX ELEVATION: 11,053 feet (3,369 m)   **AVERAGE SNOWFALL:** 400 inches (1,016 cm)
SKIABLE TERRAIN: 3,500 acres (1,420 ha)   **OPEN SKI SEASON:** November to May

They told Dave McCoy it couldn't be done. McCoy, a former California state ski champion, was advised that Mammoth Mountain, an 11,053-foot (3,369 m) lava dome located in the Eastern Sierra in Central California, was too windy, too steep, too high, and too far away from a major metropolitan area (more than 300 miles/482.8 km from both Los Angeles and San Francisco) to become a viable ski area. But McCoy, who'd spent time working in the area as a hydrographer—a job that entailed skiing up to 50 miles (80.5 km) a day to study the surrounding snowpack—had skied parts of Mammoth Mountain, knew how good it could be, and was determined to make his dream a reality. By 1953, he'd secured the permits he needed to open the ski area, using rope tows to shuttle people up the mountain. In 1955, he installed Mammoth's first chairlift.

McCoy went on to prove the doubters wrong. Skiers and snowboarders now flock en masse to Mammoth, which has expanded to more than 3,500 acres (1,420 ha) of open bowls, lazy groomers, tree skiing, and cliffy chutes, much of which, thanks to heavy snowfall (the ski area received 246 inches/ 6.3 m of snow in January 2017 alone), remains open deep into the summer. On the Fourth of July each year (assuming there's enough snow to keep skiing), visitors wearing star-spangled bikinis and swimsuits gather for a toast near the top of the mountain before ripping to the bottom of the ski area.

OPPOSITE: A skier leaves a trail of snow while skiing a run at Mammoth Mountain with the Sierra Nevada mountain range for a backdrop.

PAGES 138-139: During a blizzard at Mammoth Mountain, skiers and snow-boarders set their gear against a glass wall as they wait out the storm.

To access all that terrain, Mammoth has 25 lifts, including the Upper Panorama Gondola, which reaches to the top of the mountain (look for steam puffing out from nearby geothermal vents as you ride up) and has the distinction of being the highest chairlift in California. From the top of the gondola are views of Mammoth Lakes, a town of about 8,000 people that's rife with restaurants, bars, and natural hot springs, as well as the Minarets, toothy mountain peaks that border Yosemite National Park. Just a little way down the ridgeline from the gondola's unloading station is Dave's Run, the ski area's most popular descent, appropriately named for McCoy himself.

Also known as "Dave's Wave," since the profile of the north-facing piste resembles a large ocean wave, Dave's Run is a beloved black diamond run because west/northwest winds buff the surface into a velvety texture, allowing for smooth, high-speed turns all the way down the treeless, 42-degree, 500-vertical-foot (152.4 m) trail. The run ends at Goldhill, an easy cruiser to the Cloud Nine Express lift, or Solitude, a quick blue with access to the mid-mountain Basin Bar.

OFF THE SLOPES

Natural hot springs dot the meadows outside Mammoth Lakes and can be easily accessed via Benton Crossing Road. Some of the springs, like Pulkey's Pool and Shepherd Hot Spring, are built up with cement borders; others are left in their natural state. But all of the springs will ease your tired ski legs as you look out on the Sierra Nevada Range.

WINTER PARK RESORT

Must-Try Trail: Outhouse

MAX ELEVATION: 12,060 feet (3,675.9 m) **AVERAGE SNOWFALL:** 327 inches (830.6 cm)
SKIABLE TERRAIN: 3,081 acres (1,246 ha) **OPEN SKI SEASON:** December to April

Winter Park's Mary Jane Peak is considered a mecca for mogul skiers. That's ironic, since in 1951, Steve Bradley, who ran the ski area at the time, and George Underwood, who headed Winter Park's maintenance department, invented the first grooming machine used specifically for grooming alpine ski trails. But when Mary Jane opened for the first time in 1975, the steep and rocky terrain made most of the trails too difficult to groom, and the ski runs quickly developed moguls—and patrons loved it. Even years later, when improved grooming machines made it possible to buff out Mary Jane's terrain, diehards vigorously objected with bumper stickers on their cars that read, "'Don't Groom the Jane.'—God."

Management listened to higher powers, and today, 75 percent of the trails on Mary Jane remain ungroomed. By far the most beloved is Outhouse, so named because the outhouse for the former ski patrol shack was once located where the trail begins. At one time, to ensure that the formation of the bumps was ideal, ski patrol prevented anybody using skis shorter than 185 centimeters from going down it (the idea being short skis create smaller moguls). Today, anybody can ski or snowboard the trail, which hasn't affected the quality of the bumps. It's also allowed more people to experience the 886-vertical-foot (270 m), nearly 40-degree pitch that, thanks to its southeastern exposure, is usually bathed in sunshine.

ALTERNATIVE ROUTE

You can still experience the moguls at Winter Park without subjecting yourself to Outhouse's steeps. Over'n'Underwood is a relatively short (only 469 vertical feet/ 43 m), advanced-intermediate bump run with a moderate pitch. It skis particularly well after a big snowstorm, when powder fills in the spaces between the bumps, making for soft, bouncy turns down the slope.

A glowing sunset bathes the town nestled below Winter Park Resort.

BLUEBIRD BACKCOUNTRY

Must-Try Trail: North Face of Bear Mountain

MAX ELEVATION: 9,845 feet (3,000.8 m) **AVERAGE SNOWFALL: 280 inches (711.2 cm)**
SKIABLE TERRAIN: 1,200 acres (485.6 ha) **OPEN SKI SEASON: December to April**

When Jeff Woodward and Erik Lambert opened Bluebird Backcountry in 2019, their goal was to expose people to the thrill of backcountry skiing—trekking uphill to gain access to untouched snow—in a more controlled environment, one in which avalanche danger is low. "We wanted to take the very best from the backcountry, ski resorts, and guide services and combine them into a welcoming, convenient place for people to have a totally different kind of skiing experience," says Lambert. What Bluebird Backcountry does have: lodges, a food hut, bathrooms, instructors, backcountry rental equipment, and ski patrol. What it doesn't have: chairlifts, gondolas, or trams.

Two hours outside Denver and 40 minutes from Steamboat Springs, Bluebird Backcountry is all about easy access for skiers, right in the heart of Colorado ski country. And while it might not have the fancy infrastructure of many nearby ski resorts, it does offer a welcoming vibe.

Here's how it works. Those who are new to backcountry skiing or snowboarding can pay $199 for backcountry equipment rentals, a pass, and an instructor. "The instructor will teach people everything from how to skin uphill properly to how to use avalanche safety equipment," says Lambert. Anybody interested in taking their backcountry preparedness further can enroll in American Institute for Avalanche Research and Education (AIARE) courses,

ALTERNATIVE ROUTE

Though it's still about a mile-long (1.6 km) trek to get to, the West Bowl's 25-degree slopes offer gentler descents than those on the East Face. You'll still get to experience the fantastic views of Rabbit Ears Pass, aspen tree glades, and, of course, silky turns through powder snow.

OPPOSITE: Skiers at Bluebird Backcountry are treated to unspoiled inbounds backcountry skiing.

PAGES 144-145: Bear Mountain sits on the Continental Divide near Rabbit Ears Pass in Colorado.

which are offered throughout the season at Bluebird and teach everything from snow science (how and where avalanches are likely to form) to rescue protocol should an avalanche occur.

Experienced backcountry skiers, who must wear a transceiver and carry a shovel and probe, can make a $50 reservation and check in at the base area by simply scanning their pass, then begin trekking up the mountain on few established skin tracks. From those tracks, you can gain 1,245 feet (379.5 m) of elevation and explore 1,200 acres (485.6 ha) of skiable terrain, all of it carefully evaluated by experienced patrollers to make sure it's safe.

"We only allow 200 skiers each day we're open, which is only Thursdays through Mondays," says Lambert. "If you think about it, that's 6 acres [2.4 ha] per person and people are only taking four laps at the most, so powder gets skied out way slower than at a typical ski area."

About halfway up each skin track is a warming hut—large industrial-strength tents with space heaters—that contain a special treat for guests. "We give everybody a free slice of bacon," says

WHERE TO STAY

There's not much nearby in terms of hotels or accommodations, but visitors to Bluebird Backcountry are welcome to spend the night at a campground that's 2 miles (3.2 km) down the road from Bear Mountain in an RV, van, car, or even a tent. Those who prefer a warm bed and running water can stay 30 minutes away at Muddy Creek Cabins—log cabins situated below large buttes that tower over the rustic town of Kremmling.

ABOVE: Backcountry's nontraditional lodge structure matches its grass-roots vibe.

OPPOSITE: Bluebird Backcountry has no chairlifts; skiers and boarders make their way uphill by their own power and pre-set skin tracks.

Woodward. "After people have put in some work, they love it. It's salty and delicious and provides a ton of fuel."

The best skiers head to the summit of 9,845-foot (3,000.8 m) Bear Mountain, about a mile-long (1.6 km) trek from the base of the ski area. From the top are views of 10,115-foot (3,083.1 m) Whiteley Peak and Rabbit Ears Pass (named for two large columns of basalt rock that look like rabbit ears). On the north face of Bear Mountain is a 30-degree slope of 1,250 vertical feet (381 m). This face is mostly protected from wind and sun, so as you descend, you're likely to experience light and fluffy powder turns through snow that billows around you as you bounce through fir trees.

From the bottom, you can get back on the skin track and head up the mountain for another run. Or you can make your way to the base area, sit in front of the bonfire, and enjoy gourmet s'mores from the food hut.

MOUNT BOHEMIA

Must-Try Trail: Slide Path and Wandering Grizzly

MAX ELEVATION: 1,500 feet (457.2 m)   **AVERAGE SNOWFALL:** 273 inches (693.4 cm)
SKIABLE TERRAIN: 585 acres (236.7 ha)   **OPEN SKI SEASON:** November to May

Tree skiing? Thirty-degree steeps? Cliff drops? Chutes? Waist-deep powder? Except for the fact that the entire time you're skiing, you're staring straight at Lake Superior, you'd never believe you're in the Midwest. But believe it: Mount Bohemia, a 585-acre (236.7 ha) ski area in the northernmost part of the Upper Peninsula, is pure Michigan.

Bohemia was founded in 2000 in Lac Labelle, Michigan, an old copper mining town with a population of just over 1,000 people. The town is known for both its pasties— homemade meat pies that are *cuisine du terroir* in these parts—served up at the ski area's North Pole Bar and its expert terrain, some of which rivals Rocky Mountain descents. In fact, the skiing here is so rugged that a sign at the entrance to Mount Bohemia reads, "WARNING: NO BEGINNERS ALLOWED."

A bonus is that the trails are often covered in fresh powder. Lake-effect storms can drop 2 feet (0.6 m) of snow overnight (the ski area averages 273 inches/693.4 cm of snowfall each year), and since none of the trails are ever groomed, the possibility for face shots is abundant.

On those days, the best skiers and snowboarders head to what might be the world's only triple black diamond runs (though that rating isn't officially recognized), on a half-mile-wide (0.8 km) section of the mountain known as Extreme Backcountry (don't let the name fool you; the terrain is entirely

OPPOSITE: Mountain athletes unwind after a day on the slopes at the Nordic Spa at Mount Bohemia Ski Resort.

PAGES 150-151: Skier J. T. Robinson maneuvers through Apex Chute in the Extreme Back Country, a double black that has a vertical drop of 331 feet (100.9 m).

inbounds). That's where you'll find Slide Path and Wandering Grizzly, a linkup that features everything Mount Bohemia can throw at you.

To get to the trails, you can ride either of the ski area's two lifts (simply named Lift 1 and Lift 2) to the top of the mountain. From there, you'll make your way halfway down the mountain until you reach the top of Slide Path, a narrow couloir surrounded by bedrock basalt that requires mandatory air off a 10-foot-high (3 m) cliff band to enter. The 45-degree pitch is so steep that snow will slough off and nip at your feet as you ski down the piste. After 200 vertical feet (61 m), the trail spits out onto Wandering Grizzly, another 200 vertical feet (61 m) of 28-degree turns through gladed oaks and maples.

When you finish your run, you load onto a bus that drives you back to one of the two lifts, where you can loop around and hit some of Mount Bohemia's 105 other trails including powder runs in "The Graveyard" or glades through the Bohemia Mining Company front section of the mountain.

OFF THE SLOPES

Scandinavians settled much of the Upper Peninsula, and keeping with the Nordic tradition, the Nordic Spa was built in 2019 at Mount Bohemia. It consists of a sauna, an ice-cold pool, and a hot tub. It's believed that spending 10 to 15 minutes in a sauna, followed by a plunge in cold water, followed by a dip in a hot tub, has health benefits that include increased circulation and improved immunity.

RUBY MOUNTAINS

Must-Try Trail: The Come Line

MAX ELEVATION: 11,000 feet (3,352.8 m)   **AVERAGE SNOWFALL: 300 inches (762 cm)**
SKIABLE TERRAIN: 250,000 acres (101,171.4 ha)   **OPEN SKI SEASON: January to April**

In the early 1970s, Joe Royer was working as a ski patroller at Snowbird, Utah, and frequently drove along Interstate 80 between Salt Lake City and his hometown of Belvedere, California. Along the way, he'd gaze with awe at the Ruby Mountains, a jagged range of 10,000- to 11,000-foot (3,048-3,352.8 m) peaks that dramatically rise up from the Nevada desert. "Each time I'd drive through there I'd think, Wow, that's a big mountain range," says Royer. "I bet there could be good skiing."

In addition to ski patrolling, Royer had been doing some work with Wasatch Powderbird Guides, one of the early helicopter skiing operations in the lower 48 states. Heli-skiing appealed to him. "I liked that you're not skiing in a posse with a lot of people around, that you were exploring new terrain that hadn't been skied before, and that there was great snow," he says. So in 1977, he and two partners started Ruby Mountains Heli-Experience, using various hotels in Elko, Nevada—a town that's a mix of cowboy bars, brothels, and casinos—as the base camp. "We had only 14 guests that first year," says Royer. "And it was basically just our friends from Utah."

Since then, Ruby Mountains Heli-Experience has grown significantly. In 2017, the Royer family built a 10,000-square-foot (929 sq m) wood and stucco lodge at the base of the mountains. The lodge has 10 guest rooms, leather sofas, a stone fireplace, a hot tub, a deck that looks out at the Rubies, and a

OPPOSITE: **A helicopter follows a skier down the Come Line, one of Ruby Mountains' top runs.**

PAGES 154-155: **With 15 peaks above 11,000 feet (3,352.8 m), the Ruby Mountains are an off-the-beaten-path gem with more than 200,000 acres (494,210.8 ha) to explore.**

state-of-the-art kitchen that serves gourmet meals: seasonal flatbreads, scallops on crostini, beef swimming in a soy ginger sauce, grilled salmon with a citrus glaze, and crème brûlée with fresh berries, to name a few.

Most important, the lodge is just a two- to 10-minute flight from 250,000 acres (101,171.4 ha) of skiable terrain, where guests can take six runs, skiing or snowboarding some 12,000 vertical feet (3,657.6 m). With more than 300 inches (762 cm) of snow a year, you'll find 15 peaks to explore, offering wide open glaciated bowls, some aspen forests, and untouched terrain.

The most famous of those runs is the Come Line, a 60-foot-wide (18.3 m), 1,800-foot (548.6 m) couloir with 50-foot-high (15.2 m) walls of granite on either side and a 25- to 30-degree pitch. "We get Pacific Northwest storms, and the snow that falls by the time it gets to the Rubies is light and dry," says Royer. "And the Come Line is north facing, so it holds that good snow. The best time to ski it is around 11 in the morning in March, when the light hits it. Then you're skiing this deep powder in perfect light."

OFF THE SLOPES

After skiing, the lodge offers trapshooting, massage therapy, and live music—either a pianist playing classical music or a three-person band that covers everything from John Prine to Stevie Nicks to Bruce Springsteen. A bar serves up cocktails of your choice, and you can sip and lounge near the stone fireplace while enjoying the music.

TAOS SKI VALLEY

Must-Try Trail: Main Street

MAX ELEVATION: 12,481 feet (3,804.2 m) **AVERAGE SNOWFALL:** 300 inches (762 cm)
SKIABLE TERRAIN: 1,294 acres (523.7 ha) **OPEN SKI SEASON:** December to April

Taos Ski Valley opened in 1956, and over the years, the ski area's steep descents, tree skiing, cliffs, and chutes have become coveted terrain among serious skiers, especially those who are eager to work for their turns. Visitors to the northern New Mexico resort who are willing to shoulder their skis and hike 10 to 45 minutes—along either the West Basin Ridge or the High Line Ridge—are rewarded with hundreds of vertical feet of 30- to 45-degree lines, often covered with some of the driest, lightest powder snow you'll find anywhere on the planet (Taos averages 300 inches/762 cm of snowfall each year).

There are more technically challenging trails at Taos, but one big prize for hikers has always been Main Street, since it is the ski area's hardest trail to get to—requiring a 45-minute trek to the top of 12,481-foot (3,804.2 m) Kachina Peak, the ski area's highest point. The views from the summit of the Wheeler Wilderness Area and the Sangre de Cristo Range seem endless, and you have a good chance of spotting bighorn sheep. But it is mostly favored for its 1,053 vertical feet (320.9 m) of turns down a wide-open 35-degree slope, a significant payoff for all that toiling.

"I always felt like it was the best skiing you could do without a helicopter," says Dave Hahn, a longtime Taos ski patroller and ski guide who has summitted Mount Everest 15 times.

OPPOSITE: Snowboarders take a lesson from a Taos Ski Valley instructor down a groomed run.

PAGES 158-159: The John Dunn Shops in Taos's historic district offer 18 retail stores, galleries, boutiques, and dining in one beautiful location.

Very little has changed at Taos since it opened—après-ski libations on the deck of the Hotel St. Bernard have been a tradition since 1960—but in 2014, a chairlift was installed that allows skiers and snowboarders to zip to the top of Main Street in just five minutes. Of course, the installation of a chairlift also made hitting Main Street a lot easier to the everyday skier and snowboarder looking to tackle the trail without the hike. That enlarged footprint also changed the complexion of the trail. Now you're likely to find a long mogul run, but the changes didn't render Main Street any less great. "It makes it more challenging because you're not just floating through powder down it," says Hahn.

But the best way to ski Main Street is still the old-fashioned way: hiking up to it and skiing down in deep powder. To do that, you need to hit the ski area a day or two after a storm.

"At times, before the ski area opens the lift, they'll open the trail to hikers," says Hahn. "If that's the case, it's worth it to hike up it so that you can ski waist-deep snow on perfect, rolling terrain."

ALTERNATIVE ROUTE

Despite its rugged reputation, nearly half of all the terrain at Taos is beginner or intermediate. That includes Porcupine, a gentle trail with some steep roll-overs that's typically groomed and has brilliant views of the surrounding mountains. There are two picnic tables along the trail at different locations—perfect for enjoying a packed lunch on a sunny day (the ski area averages 285 sunny days each year).

WHITEFACE MOUNTAIN RESORT

Must-Try Trail: Skyward

MAX ELEVATION: 4,650 feet (1,417.3 m)
SKIABLE TERRAIN: 288 acres (116.5 ha)
AVERAGE SNOWFALL: 180 inches (457.2 cm)
OPEN SKI SEASON: November to April

With 51 lift-serviced mountains, New York has more ski areas than any other state in the United States (by comparison, Colorado has 31). Most of those ski areas are small, but Whiteface Mountain Resort, near the Adirondack town of Lake Placid, is world class. The ski area's trails are so long and steep, in fact, that they were worthy of hosting alpine ski racing at the 1980 Winter Olympics. Today, the entire Lake Placid area serves as a sort of shrine to those games, and at Whiteface, where Olympic rings are ubiquitous, you can still push out of the start houses used for the alpine racing events.

"Those Olympics are best known for the U.S. hockey team's win against the Soviet Union—the 'Miracle on Ice'—and Eric Heiden's accomplishments in speed skating, but the ski racing was great," says Andrew Weibrecht, a former member of the U.S. Ski Team who grew up near Whiteface and won silver and bronze at the 2014 and 2010 Olympics, respectively. "It was probably the first time a lot of people in the United States were exposed to ski racing at such a high level and at such high speeds."

Skyward, the trail used for the women's downhill race, is also one of Whiteface's best recreational ski trails. Beginning near the ski area's 4,867-foot (1,483.5 m) summit (Whiteface is the fifth highest mountain in New York State), the trail overlooks the billion-year-old Great Range and Lake Champlain on

OPPOSITE: Whiteface Mountain's slopes are shrouded in a morning Adirondack mist.

PAGES 162-163: Whiteface Mountain is the fifth highest peak in New York State; its summit hits 4,650 feet (1,417.3 m) in elevation.

the Vermont border and wends through a large corridor of evergreens for nearly 2,000 vertical feet (609.6 m). "The first two-thirds of the trail is really wide open and has a nice, steep sustained pitch," says Weibrecht. "It's the quintessential trail for making long-radius, fast turns."

The optimal conditions for opening the throttle on Skyward present themselves in the morning in midwinter, when the trail is groomed and frigid temperatures freeze the corduroy into a hard, fast surface. But be warned: the dead of winter in upstate New York can be brutal. In February 2016, temperatures dipped to minus 114°F (−81.11°C) atop Whiteface. Skyward also skis well in the spring, when the sun cooks the snow into a soft, granular surface. "My most memorable spring skiing was when I was a kid," says Weibrecht. "The mountain was supposed to close, and then it snowed 84 inches [2.1 m], so they stayed open. The sun came out and warmed everything up. It was like being on the beach but getting to ski. We lapped Skyward over and over for a week."

WHERE TO STAY

The Weibrecht family bought the Mirror Lake Inn—situated on Mirror Lake and within walking distance of the town of Lake Placid—in 1976. Each guest room faces the mountains and the lake (part of which is cleared for ice-skating). The fine-dining restaurant serves five-course meals; the spa offers an array of treatments, including an "Adirondack maple sugar body scrub"; and there's an on-site ski shop—exclusive to the inn's guests—that provides rental gear and tuning for skis and snowboards.

ALTA SKI AREA

Must-Try Trail: Alf's High Rustler

MAX ELEVATION: 11,068 feet (3,373.5 m)   **AVERAGE SNOWFALL:** 547 inches (1,389.4 cm)
SKIABLE TERRAIN: 2,614 acres (1,057.9 ha)   **OPEN SKI SEASON:** November to April

It's printed right on Utah's license plates: "Greatest Snow on Earth." That might sound like hyperbole, but there's science to back up the claim. In 1962, Edward LaChapelle, an avalanche researcher, mountaineer, and skier, wrote that "the best deep-powder skiing is not found in the lightest snow, but rather in snow with enough 'body' to provide good flotation for the running ski." According to Jim Steenburgh, a professor of atmospheric sciences at the University of Utah, these optimal conditions are achieved when storms generate at least 10 inches (25.4 cm) of snow, producing flakes that become gradually less dense, so that lower-density snow sits on top of higher-density snow.

"Those are ideal circumstances for ski flotation," he says. "And because storms in Utah often start out warm and become gradually colder, they bring in high-density snow followed by low-density snow. So these types of storms occur frequently in Utah's Wasatch Mountains."

No other ski area in Utah benefits more from these snowstorms than Alta. Since the ski area, about 40 minutes from Salt Lake City, sits at the dead end of Little Cottonwood Canyon, the storms become trapped in the surrounding mountains, dropping an average of 547 inches (1,389.4 cm) of snow on Alta's faces each year. More important, the ski area experiences a powder day—when at least 10 inches (25.4 cm) of snow falls in a single storm—about 17 times

APRÈS SKI

The Peruvian Bar, which locals call the "P Dog," is known for its microbrews, free popcorn appetizers, and frat-house-like atmosphere, aided by an amalgam of low-rent furnishings: cheap leather couches; mounted bighorn sheep, bison, and black bear; and other random memorabilia.

OPPOSITE: Professional skier Sam Cohen plows through deep powder on Alf's High Rustler during a winter storm in Alta.

PAGES 166-167: A crowd gathers on top of Alf's High Rustler during Alta's closing day festivities.

a season (November to April), or about once every 10 days.

On those powder days, one of the first trails skiers head to is Alf's High Rustler, a 45-degree, 1,000-vertical-foot (304.8 m) descent that's been coveted by skiers for more than 100 years. Beginning in 1920, intrepid backcountry skiers from the Wasatch Mountain Club would trek from nearby Brighton to ski the "high part" of the face on what was then known as Rustler Hill, the name given to the peak by the silver miners who occupied the area from around 1865 into the early 20th century.

By the early 1930s, the U.S. Forest Service had taken control of the area and, with the popularity of skiing growing throughout the country, commissioned Alf Engen, a skiing legend from Norway, to see if the terrain above the town of Alta might make for a good ski area. In 1939, Alta opened to the public, and High Rustler was one of the first named trails. In 1978, High Rustler was renamed Alf's High Rustler in honor of Engen.

ALTERNATIVE ROUTE

You can experience Alta's magical powder skiing without subjecting yourself to 45-degree steeps. By riding the Wildcat Chairlift, a slow double chair, you can access Johnson's Warm Up, an open, treeless face with a short 25-degree pitch. If that feels good, ride the same lift and try Wildcat Bowl, a slightly steeper trail with open glades.

ABOVE: Alta's Rustler Lodge offers comfortable seating for a break from the challenging terrain.

OPPOSITE: Pro skier Dan Treadway takes on fresh powder in Alta's scenic backcountry.

Alf's High Rustler, which overlooks the tiny village of Alta and the 11,000-foot-plus (3,352.8 m) peaks that surround it, is considered one of the most challenging, and therefore one of the most famous, trails in North America. "In powder, this run can change your life," says Todd Ligare, a pro skier who grew up in Utah. "There's just something magical about the combination of its well-protected north aspect, consistent pitch, and unusually magnetic fall line that invites you in for a fluid, high-speed, top-to-bottom ride."

Around the end of April, the top of Alf's High Rustler also hosts the ski area's closing day party, when hundreds of skiers dress in costumes and, if conditions line up, blast music, dance, and imbibe under the springtime sun. As dusk approaches, everybody skis the trail's steep, slushy moguls back to the base of the mountain.

PARK CITY MOUNTAIN RESORT

Must-Try Trail: 94 Turns

MAX ELEVATION: 10,026 feet (3,055.9 m)   **AVERAGE SNOWFALL: 355 inches (901.7 cm)**
SKIABLE TERRAIN: 7,300+ acres (2,954.2+ ha)   **OPEN SKI SEASON: November to April**

I n 2015, Park City Mountain Resort merged with Canyons Resort, combining 7,300 acres (2,954.2 ha) and becoming the largest ski area in the United States. Among that terrain are the trails on Ninety-Nine 90, so named because the peak is 9,990 feet (2,770.6 m) high. The skiing off the summit is an expert's dream: everything from open faces to chutes to tree skiing to serious steeps. But the signature trail here is 94 Turns, a wide-open 36-degree descent. (Supposedly, the trail requires 94 turns to get from top to bottom; go ahead and count for yourself.)

To get to the trail, you take the Ninety-Nine 90 Express quad that drops you off near the top of the peak. From here, it's worth the five- to 10-minute hike to the very top of Ninety-Nine 90 so that you can peer out past the ski area boundary into Big Cottonwood Canyon and at some of the Wasatch Mountains' 10,000- and 11,000-foot (3,048 and 3,352.8 m) peaks.

Once you ski back down to 94 Turns, you're likely to find a trail full of moguls. The consistent pitch makes for a fun bump run, but it truly shines when covered by several inches of fresh snow, so try to nail it on a powder day—and try to get first tracks. That might require waiting in the lift line while employees mitigate avalanche danger (Ninety-Nine 90 typically opens later than the rest of the mountain during heavy snowfall), but the payoff is worth it: powder snow that billows over your head for 800 vertical feet (243.8 m).

CULTURAL IMMERSION

The town of Park City has a history rich in precious metals. Silver was discovered in 1868, and you can still ski right past several mines in the ski area. One of those claims, the Ontario Mine, was purchased by George Hearst, the father of William Randolph Hearst, and partners for $27,000 in 1872. It would go on to earn more than $50 million.

A skier navigates from the Upper Face to Dutch Hollow, an alternate route to 94 Turns, off the Ninety-Nine 90 Express chairlift.

POWDER MOUNTAIN

Must-Try Trail: Carpe Diem to Big Kash

MAX ELEVATION: 9,422 feet (2,871.8 m) **AVERAGE SNOWFALL:** 500+ inches (1,270+ cm)
SKIABLE TERRAIN: 8,464 acres (3,425.3 ha) **OPEN SKI SEASON:** December to April

Going to Powder Mountain, located about 50 miles (80.5 km) north of Salt Lake City, Utah, is a bit like taking a trip into the past. There's no faux Bavarian village with boutique ski shops and fancy dining here, and much of the infrastructure that does exist is wonderfully dated. The ski area's two small day lodges were built in the 1970s, and with cafeterias that serve greasy fries and burgers and communal dining picnic tables (many of the people eating lunch are locals), they retain the charm of that era. Though some of the chairlifts have been upgraded over the years, there's still a slow double chair, and upon finishing several different runs, you need to hop on a bus in order to get back to the lifts.

The ski area is massive. According to many, Powder Mountain, with 8,464 acres (3,425.3 ha) of skiable terrain, is the biggest ski area in North America. But because only 2,800 acres (1,133.1 ha) of that is lift-served skiing and snowboarding—another 5,464 acres (2,211.2 ha) of inbounds, avalanche-controlled terrain is accessible only by hiking or by a ride in a snowcat—that claim is disputed. (Most ski areas are measured by the amount of lift-served terrain.)

What's indisputable is this: True to its name, you can almost always find powder skiing at Powder Mountain. The ski area receives an average of 500

OPPOSITE: A lone skier leaves fresh tracks in the fresh powder on Carpe Diem, located on James Peak—the tallest peak at Powder Mountain.

PAGES 174-175: A snowboarder traverses Carpe Diem during a fresh powder day.

inches (12.7 m) of snow each year, and storms that blow in often dump a foot (0.3 m) of snow or more during a 24-hour period. Because it doesn't get the massive crowds that better known Utah ski areas in Park City and Little Cottonwood Canyon do and because there's plenty of terrain to go around, it can take days, even up to a week, for the trails to get totally tracked out. "It's a unique characteristic of Powder," says Nicky Keefer, a pro skier who grew up skiing at Powder Mountain. "You can almost always find deep snow—especially if you're willing to hike a little bit."

That's the case with Carpe Diem and Big Kash, two trails that combine for nearly 3,000 vertical feet (914.4 m) of skiing. Because you have to take a five-minute ride in a snowcat and then hike 20 minutes to the top of James Peak (at 9,422 feet/ 2,871.8 m, the highest point at the ski area) to get to the trail, the terrain gets very little traffic. Therefore, the descent—an abundance of 30-degree open faces, sparse glades, and gullies—is typically filled with light, dry snow. "We call it 'cold smoke,'" says Keefer. "And it's flying into our faces and filling our lungs the whole way down."

APRÈS SKI

About 20 minutes from the ski area in the small town of Huntsville is the Shooting Star Saloon, which was established in 1879 and bills itself as the "oldest continuously operating Saloon west of the Mississippi." Inside are a stuffed Saint Bernard head on the wall, hundreds of dollar bills stapled to the ceiling, and double-patty, bacon-filled cheeseburgers.

SNOWBIRD SKI RESORT

Must-Try Trail: Great Scott

MAX ELEVATION: 11,000 feet (3,352.8 m)   **AVERAGE SNOWFALL:** 500 inches (1,270 cm)
SKIABLE TERRAIN: 2,500 acres (1,011.7 ha)   **OPEN SKI SEASON:** December to May

If it weren't for Fitzhugh Scott, Snowbird might never have existed. In the mid-1960s, the wealthy Milwaukee, Wisconsin-based architect—and die-hard skier—provided Ted Johnson, the general manager at Alta Ski Area's Alta Lodge, the money needed to buy the Snowbird Mining Claim just down the road from Alta. (Snowbird now sits on what was once known as the Emma Mine—namesake for the ski area's Big Emma run in Snowbird's Gad Valley today. It produced more than $3.8 million in silver when it was active, one of the largest producers of silver ore in the Wasatch Mountains.) When Johnson and cofounder Dick Bass opened Snowbird to the public in 1971, they honored Scott by naming one of the steepest trails on the mountain after him.

Great Scott, which starts atop a large cirque near the mountain's 11,000-foot-high peak (3,352.8 m), is considered Snowbird's most famous trail—Hollywood famous, in fact. In 1985, it was featured in the cult classic *Better Off Dead,* in a scene in which the main character, Lane Myer (played by John Cusack), tries to win back his estranged girlfriend by skiing down the fearsome K-12 (played by Great Scott). He falls and tumbles all the way down it.

Though challenging, skiing Great Scott isn't quite as difficult as Lane Myer would make it seem, especially when it's full of powder, which is often the case. Snowbird is tucked into Little Cottonwood Canyon, a large ravine above Salt Lake City that traps storms. When that happens, it can snow for several

APRÈS SKI

SeventyOne (named for the year the ski area opened), looks like the inside of a retro '70s diner right down to its old ski posters and disco-era wallpaper. As you look back up at the ski area, you can sip on draft beers and cocktails and snack on soft pretzels and ahi tuna nachos.

OPPOSITE: The heated pool at the Cliff Lodge in Snowbird offers relaxation with mountain views.

PAGES 178-179: Snowbird's Aerial Tram first opened in 1971 and continues to whisk passengers to the summit in 10 minutes.

NO DIVING

days, resulting in 4 to 5 feet (1.2-1.5 m) of accumulation (Snowbird averages 500 inches/1,270 cm of snow each winter). On occasion, that causes visitors to the ski area to be interlodged, which means they're not allowed to leave the concrete, avalanche-proof hotels that line the base of the resort. Powerful fronts can interlodge guests for several days while avalanche mitigation crews make the mountain safe.

Roads to the resort can also be shut down to inbound (and outbound) traffic for days while avalanche mitigation work takes place, so plan ahead if you're looking to catch first tracks on a fresh powder day.

Once the ski area reopens, most skiers and snowboarders head to the aerial tram, a 100-person lift that carries people 2,900 vertical feet (883.9 m) from the bottom of the mountain all the way to the summit.

"Riding up the tram, Great Scott is the one prominent run that's right in your face," says Ty Peterson, a professional skier who grew up skiing at Snowbird. "And when you're standing at the top

WHERE TO STAY

Driving up to Snowbird in the morning from Salt Lake City or the surrounding suburbs can be an infuriating slog through bumper-to-bumper traffic. That's one of the reasons you'll be happy to stay at the Cliff Lodge. Walking distance from the chairlifts, the Cliff has an on-site ski rental and repair shop and complimentary ski lockers, an outdoor pool and hot tubs, and a full-service spa.

of the trail and the tram is passing overhead, you're thinking, *Well, I better give the people watching a good show.*"

To do that, you first have to navigate through rocks and moguls. "Getting into Great Scott is the hardest part," says Peterson. "But that's a good thing because it deters a lot of people from skiing it." Once you've made it through the entrance, the 40-degree run fans out into a north-facing, open bowl that can be wind-blown and chalky; in early summer, full of corn snow (Snowbird is often able to stay open until June or even July); or a powder paradise.

"There was one day when I woke up at six in the morning and the snow report said that 8 inches [20.3 cm] had fallen overnight," says Peterson. "By the time I got up to the mountain a few hours later it had snowed another 8 inches [20.3 cm]. I dropped in and it was just the deepest turns. I got to the bottom and just had the biggest smile."

STOWE MOUNTAIN RESORT

Must-Try Trail: Goat

MAX ELEVATION: 4,395 feet (1,339.6 m) **AVERAGE SNOWFALL:** 314 inches (797.6 cm)
SKIABLE TERRAIN: 485 acres (196.3 ha) **OPEN SKI SEASON:** November to April

According to local legend, Goat got its name when a hiker, attempting to trek up what would become the trail, quipped that only a mountain goat would be able to climb its dicey terrain. Sometime after that, in 1960, the brass at Stowe Mountain—opened in 1934—created Goat, cutting a narrow strip through the evergreens and maples (the trail was known as Chamois until 1962). Those who dared tackle it made a quick discovery: it was even harder to ski down it than it was to hike up it.

Today, Goat is still considered one of the most challenging trails in New England. It's a winding, 2,400-foot (731.5 m) descent with 36-degree steeps, ledges, boulders, and streams that run right through the middle of the trail. And just in case the obstacles aren't enough of a challenge, Goat is frequently bumped up with moguls or glazed with ice—or both. Burning quads are a guarantee, so frequent stops are a must, which gives skiers a chance to take in the scenery: New Hampshire's White Mountains to the east and Smugglers' Notch, famous for being part of the Underground Railroad, to the north.

After Goat has thoroughly beaten skiers down, the town of Stowe is there to comfort them. Just 15 minutes from the ski area, Stowe is the 250-year-old Vermont town that you thought existed only in movies—a Norman Rockwell vision of white church steeples, red barns, and penny candy stores. There's also a plethora of restaurants, hotels, and the Stoweflake hotel's full-service spa.

WHERE TO STAY

For a unique experience, book the Stone Hut at the top of Stowe Mountain. Built in 1936, the rustic hut has bunk beds and is heated with a wood stove (you'll need to bring a sleeping bag and food). Best of all, if you stay there on a night it snows, you're guaranteed early-morning powder turns down Goat before anybody else.

The spire of the iconic Stowe Community Church rises against Vermont's Green Mountains after a snowfall.

MAD RIVER GLEN

Must-Try Trail: Paradise

MAX ELEVATION: 3,637 feet (1,108.6 m) **AVERAGE SNOWFALL:** 228 inches (579.1 cm)
SKIABLE TERRAIN: 915 acres (370.3 ha) **OPEN SKI SEASON:** Mid-December to mid-April

Mad River Glen's 34-year-old slogan is printed on bumper stickers that are pasted on cars, lift shacks, and restrooms throughout the world: "Ski It If You Can." It's an appropriate challenge, since the narrow slopes of the northern Vermont mountain are an obstacle course of tight trees, rocks, and ice, only a small portion of which are ever groomed. As one of only three areas in the United States that doesn't allow snowboarding (Alta and Deer Valley in Utah are the others), ski it you must.

If you do accept the challenge, you might as well go big—and Paradise, a 38-degree, 794-vertical-foot (242 m) trail, tosses everything Mad River has to offer at skiers. Founded in 1948, the ski area is a throwback to ski days of yore. To get to Paradise, for instance, you must ride 10 minutes to the summit on Lift 1, the only single-person chairlift left in the lower 48.

From the top of the lift, you sidestep up to the Fall Line trail, where you'll make a few turns down before veering onto Paradise. The first part of the run is actually a mellow summer hiking path that's part of the Long Trail, a 273-mile (439.4 km) route that runs north and south through the entire state of Vermont. In winter and on skis, it becomes a narrow, fast luge track along the mountain's ridgeline. From there, you're forced to descend an 8-foot-high (2.4 m) ice ledge before making your way through oddly spaced and shaped moguls and, eventually, a thicket of maples and pines.

ALTERNATIVE ROUTE

Skiing Chute and Liftline, the two trails underneath Lift 1, gives you the very Mad River opportunity to be heckled or cheered by chairlift riders. It also allows you to ski nearly 2,000 vertical feet (609.6 m) of 30-degree moguls, challenging yet slightly less technical terrain than what you'll find on Paradise.

Skiers make their way down Mad River Glen's most difficult marked trail, Paradise, which is steep and narrow.

KILLINGTON SKI RESORT

Must-Try Trail: Outer Limits

MAX ELEVATION: 4,241 feet (1,292.7 m)   **AVERAGE SNOWFALL:** 250 inches (635 cm)
SKIABLE TERRAIN: 1,509 acres (610.7 ha)   **OPEN SKI SEASON:** November to May

In 1979, when Killington Mountain Resort expanded to nearby Bear Mountain, trail builders created one of the most famous mogul runs in the world. "What makes Outer Limits so great is that it's wide—two football fields wide—there are moguls wall to wall, and there's a perfect, sustained pitch for 1,200 vertical feet [365.8 m]," says Donna Weinbrecht, who grew up skiing at Killington and won the gold medal in the moguls competition at the 1992 Winter Olympics. "It's the run that made me a champion."

Killington has continued to expand and now has 1,509 skiable acres (610.7 ha), making it the largest ski area in New England. But despite its growth, Outer Limits remains the ski area's most popular trail, mainly because it's formidable. Skiers who take on the slope, which has a pitch of 27 degrees, are typically forced to negotiate oddly spaced bumps that can grow nearly as large as Volkswagen Beetles and are often glazed with ice. "I've skied them when they're rock hard," says Weinbrecht. "But that's part of the challenge."

The optimal time to ski Outer Limits is in the spring, when the sun cooks the snow into a slosh and skiers can pound down through soft mounds of granular corn snow. On those days, the trail becomes something of a main stage. As skiers make their way down the piste, they'll often hear hollers of encouragement from people riding the Bear Mountain Express Chairlift and from revelers on the deck of the Bear Mountain Lodge.

APRÈS SKI

The Wobbly Barn is an institution. Opened in 1963, the bar and restaurant look like an old Vermont barn from the outside and a dance party on the inside, complete with concert lighting and loud music spun by a DJ or played by a live band. A word of warning: You might wander in for an après drink and wander out six hours later, still in your ski clothes.

Killington offers 155 marked trails to skiers and snowboarders, many with sweeping panoramic views of the ski area.

MOUNT BAKER SKI AREA

Must-Try Trail: Gabl's

MAX ELEVATION: 5,000 feet (1,524 m)   **AVERAGE SNOWFALL:** 688 inches (1,747.5 cm)
SKIABLE TERRAIN: 1,000 acres (404.7 ha)   **OPEN SKI SEASON:** November to April

No other ski area in the world gets more snow than Mount Baker. The remote northwest Washington locale averages 688 inches (1,747.5 cm) of snow each year (the 1998–99 ski season was a white-out, setting a world record of 1,140 inches/2,895.6 cm of snowfall in a single season). The unusually high amount of precipitation is mostly due to its favorable geographic position. "It sits out on the northwestern edge of the Cascade Range," says Edward Blanchard-Wrigglesworth, a professor of atmospheric sciences at the University of Washington. "So it's more exposed to any storm with a westerly component, which is the most common type of storm. Being close to the Salish Sea doesn't hurt either—more moisture equals more precipitation."

Although the ski area wasn't officially established until 1953, earlier skiers couldn't stay away from all that snow. In the 1920s, a narrow, windy road—part of the Mount Baker Highway, which begins about 55 miles (88.5 km) away in Bellingham, Washington—was constructed. It ended at what's now one of the base areas for the Mount Baker Ski Area. At first, skiers trekked up the mountain to find powder turns. By 1937, a makeshift cable pulley surface lift had been installed. And though the area has evolved quite a bit since then, the infrastructure remains relatively small. Patrons still drive the somewhat treacherous road to the ski area—snowbanks act as guardrails—and there's

OPPOSITE: Mount Baker offers mountain enthusiasts more than 1,000 acres (404.7 ha) of skiable terrain.

PAGES 190-191: With headlamps to guide their way, Mount Baker's Pro Patrol head out before the sun for early avalanche control.

no lodging, fancy dining, or boutique shops. "Mount Baker is not about the condos or heated sidewalks," says Colin Wiseman, content director for the *Snowboarder's Journal*. "It's all about the skiing and snowboarding."

The biggest investments at Mount Baker have been those made to improve the on-piste experience. Eight four-person chairlifts and two handle tows now access 1,000 acres (404.7 ha) of terrain across three peaks—the highest standing at 5,000 feet (1,524 m) above sea level.

And when it storms, locals in the know head straight to Chair 5 to ski the double black, Gabl's. "It has that perfect mix of terrain," says Wiseman. "A steep pitch that you can make fast turns down, gullies that you can slash in and out of, shelves to catch air off at the top, and a little stack of pillows that you can pop through near the bottom."

As skiers and snowboarders descend 1,112 vertical feet (338.9 m) on Gabl's, they're likely to hear hoots of encouragement coming from people riding the lift. "On a powder day, it's a scene," says Wiseman. "Everybody is hucking and putting on a show."

ALTERNATIVE ROUTE

You don't need to take on steeps and gullies to enjoy the powder at Mount Baker. Austin, a trail located off Chair 1, near the ski area's border with the Mount Baker–Snoqualmie National Forest, is a wide-open run with a moderate, consistent pitch that descends 554 vertical feet (168.9 m).

CRYSTAL MOUNTAIN

Must-Try Trail: Powder Bowl

MAX ELEVATION: 7,012 feet (2,137.3 m)   **AVERAGE SNOWFALL:** 486 inches (1,234.4 cm)
SKIABLE TERRAIN: 2,600 acres (1,052.2 ha)   **OPEN SKI SEASON:** October to July

Crystal Mountain, located at the end of a dead-end road in central Washington, is known for its steep terrain, cliffs, couloirs, tree skiing, and front-and-center views of Mount Rainier, a 14,411-foot-high (4,392.5 m) volcano that's the highest peak in the state. It's not known for its lodging, which is limited. As a result, the ski area has developed a serious motor-home culture. Visitors to Crystal often drive their RVs, souped-up vans, or campers to the mountain and park in lot B for the weekend—or longer—sitting around bonfires, drinking and eating, skiing the resort's 2,600 acres (1,052.2 ha) of terrain, and waiting for a major snowstorm to hit.

When that happens, skiers and snowboarders flock to Powder Bowl, which more than lives up to its name. Crystal averages 486 inches (1,234.4 cm) of snow each year, and since Powder Bowl is located at the top of the mountain the snow that falls on its flanks is dry and light. What's more, southwest winds scrape snow off other parts of the mountain and deposit it into the basin, making for substantially deeper powder turns. And since the bowl is shaded, that deep, light, dry snow holds for several days after a storm.

There are many ways into the bowl, but the best approach is to ski it straight off the top, right down the gut. That line will allow you to milk all 581 vertical feet of the bowl, enjoying the 35- to 40-degree pitch as snow puffs up around you.

APRÈS SKI

The Snorting Elk Cellar brings a bit of Bavaria to Washington State. The Rathskeller-style bar serves locally brewed beers and is well known for its homemade cookies and pizza. Its annual events are also beloved, including the amateur ski and snowboard film night (movies shot by people using GoPros and phones), and the Retro Ski Wear Party.

A skier somersaults off a rock formation, soaring above the slopes of Crystal Mountain.

WHISTLER BLACKCOMB

Must-Try Trail: Secret Bowl to Secret Chute

MAX ELEVATION: 7,494 feet (2,284 m)   **AVERAGE SNOWFALL: 448 inches (1,138 cm)**
SKIABLE TERRAIN: 8,171 acres (3,306.7 ha)   **OPEN SKI SEASON: November to May**

Even 25 years after the run was established, the Secret Bowl—carved deep into Blackcomb Peak's high alpine, obscured from view by large bands of rock—is still a seldom-skied chunk of terrain, a haven from the ski area's crowds and a prime source of powder stashes.

"When we discovered it in 1980, there was no lift service up there," says Arthur DeJong, a former ski patrol manager and mountain operations manager for Blackcomb. "We kind of stumbled into this little bowl and discovered some of the best skiing. To be honest, we ski patrollers wanted to keep it secret because the skiing was so good in there." In 1985, a T-bar was installed, allowing paying customers to access the bowl. Two years later, the Seventh Heaven Express chairlift was erected, providing even easier access. "But it still requires a traverse to get there," says DeJong, "and for whatever reason, it's still mostly overlooked."

For the lucky skiers who do discover the bowl, they'll often find it full of powder. Located near the top of the mountain, just below Horstman Glacier—a remnant of the massive glaciers that molded these volcanic peaks into perfect ski slopes—the bowl is a catcher's mitt for westerly and southwesterly winds, which snatch snow from other parts of the mountain and load the 30-degree pitch with deep powder. (If it's raining at the base of the mountain, as is often the case at Whistler Blackcomb, chances are it's snowing

OPPOSITE: **Find a luxurious stay and a plush lobby at the Four Seasons Resort Whistler.**

PAGES 196-197: **Professional skier Wiley Miller takes flight in the fresh powder of Whistler backcountry.**

fresh flakes up in the high alpine, where Secret Bowl is located.)

Once you drop into the bowl, the ski area's infrastructure completely disappears from sight and hearing, making it feel as though you're descending a remote backcountry slope. After bounding through approximately 850 vertical feet (259 m) of deep snow, farming fresh tracks throughout the 200-yard-wide (182.8 m) basin, you exit the bowl to the right, through Secret Chute. This is where the trail becomes more difficult.

The narrow shaft, framed by high walls of black rock on either side, is 535 vertical feet (163 m) long and has a 40-degree pitch. "It's north facing, so the snow can be even lighter in there," says DeJong. "When I was a patroller and nobody knew about it, it was one of my favorite places to ski. People still don't really know about it, and it's a great way to finish an incredible run."

The chute dumps you out at Glacier Drive, where you can hop the Glacier Express lift to the Showcase T-Bar and access to the entrance of Blackcomb Glacier.

ALTERNATIVE ROUTE

You don't need to take on 40-degree steeps to ski above the tree line on Blackcomb Peak. In fact, most of the terrain off the Seventh Heaven Express chairlift is inter-mediate skiing. One of the best runs is Hugh's Heaven, a 1,843-vertical-foot (562 m) descent down groomed trail with views of Whistler Mountain.

RED MOUNTAIN RESORT

Must-Try Trail: Powder Fields

MAX ELEVATION: 6,807 feet (2,075 m) **AVERAGE SNOWFALL:** 300 inches (762 cm)
SKIABLE TERRAIN: 3,850 acres (1,558 ha) **OPEN SKI SEASON:** December to April

You can't trust the snow report at RED Mountain. Located in the West Kootenay region of British Columbia, just north of the American border, the resort allegedly receives only 300 inches (762 cm) of snowfall each season. And, according to meteorological reports, big storms drop only about 10 inches (25.4 cm) of snow on the flanks of the ski area. But locals will tell you that's just not true. Storms at RED seem to last for days, and favorable winds tend to scoop up the light, dry flakes and deposit them on certain aspects, making for waist-deep turns on a number of the ski area's trails.

Until somewhat recently, RED's reputation for good powder skiing was a fairly well-kept secret. In fact, skiers, many of them Scandinavian miners drawn to the region during the 1890 gold rush, began trekking up and noodling down RED Mountain toward the end of the 19th century. The ski area was the first in western Canada to have a chairlift, which was constructed in 1947 on the 5,220-foot (1,591.1 m) cone-shaped peak. Some years later, it expanded to include Granite Mountain, a 6,807-foot (2,075 m) peak that's adjacent to RED. And in 2013, it grew again, adding 6,719-foot-high (2,048 m) Grey Mountain, a 1,000-acre (404.7 ha) addition full of ridgelines and natural half-pipes that, at the time, was the biggest ski area expansion in North America in 40 years.

OPPOSITE: RED Mountain is built around a former gold mining town in the Kootenay region of British Columbia.

PAGES 200-201: With freshly fallen snow to explore, a snowboarder makes first tracks on a woodsy run.

With that, RED Mountain Resort ballooned to 3,850 acres (1,558 ha) of skiable terrain—and offers a total drop of 2,919 vertical feet (889.7 m)—making it one of the largest ski areas in North America. That, along with improvements to the small village's lodging and dining scene—in 2018, the Josie, a luxury boutique hotel and spa opened slope-side—have garnered the resort quite a bit more attention.

These days, sizable crowds of skiers and snowboarders descend upon five different peaks and 119 marked ski trails. RED also offers cat skiing—for $10 a ride—on the flanks of neighboring Mount Kirkup. Most visitors are drawn to the area in hopes of experiencing some deep powder turns on the challenging slopes and the chance to make fresh tracks.

"RED is a really playful mountain," says Dane Tudor, a pro skier who grew up skiing at the resort. "It doesn't have a ton of vertical drop, but it has lots of advanced tree skiing and steeps."

Despite the increased crowds, you can still find fresh tracks at the ski resort. That's even true on

APRÈS SKI

Rafters, an always packed bar in the upstairs of the base lodge, is regarded by many as one of the best après-ski scenes in North America. Nineteenth-century mine timbers frame the space, and the walls are a shrine to skiers and ski culture. At long tables, patrons chow on heaping piles of nachos, drink from pitchers of beer, and on occasion play drinking games.

the trail that has been lauded by the skiing community as one of the best inbounds powder runs in North America, the aptly named Powder Fields. Located on Granite Peak, the approximately 700-vertical-foot (213.4 m), moderately pitched trail is often full of deep stashes of snow tucked between well-spaced trees.

Though the trail has sections of expert terrain—lines that were hairy enough to host the Red Bull Cold Rush, a big mountain skiing competition that features athletes who spend as much time in the air as they do on the snow—almost anybody can ski it.

"You'll see the young bucks throwing flips off the 30-foot-high [9.1 m] Orchard Cliffs," says Tudor. "But for the most part, it's a nice powder run with little pillow lines and mostly mellow terrain for all abilities. Your grandparents can ski down it."

ABOVE: RED Mountain has six chairlifts and two surface lifts to transport skiers to more than 110 named runs.

OPPOSITE: Pro skier and powder bum Zack Giffin launches from a powdery cliff at RED Mountain.

SANGRIDA AND MISTA PEAKS

Must-Try Trail: Sundog

MAX ELEVATION: 7,545 feet (2,300 m)   **AVERAGE SNOWFALL:** 360 inches (914.4 cm)
SKIABLE TERRAIN: 21,500 acres (8,700.7 ha)   **OPEN SKI SEASON:** December to mid-April

When the snowcat was invented in the early 1900s, it's unlikely anybody imagined that the utilitarian machine, mainly used to ferry people who lived in very snowy, icy locales, would someday transform into tank-tracked party buses—complete with soft leather seating and booming sound systems— and be used to transport skiers and snowboarders into the backcountry to bomb down steep, deep powder runs. These days, the capital of snow- cat skiing is British Columbia, where some 20 operations shuttle people to hundreds of thousands of acres of chutes, open bowls, well-spaced trees, and powder pillow lines. Among the most respected of those oper- ations is Baldface Valhalla, which offers day trips (a much cheaper option than many of the snowcat skiing outfits that require you to throw down for a week-long stay at their backcountry lodge).

Founded in 2001 outside Nelson, British Columbia, the company (previ- ously known as Valhalla Powdercats) employs two 12-passenger cats and a 14-passenger cat that are all equipped to power up the gnarliest ascents. "They climb really steep faces and get you into things you couldn't otherwise access," says Tyler Towes, the lead guide at Baldface Valhalla. During the winter, this part of the Selkirk Mountains averages between 300 and 360 inches of snow each year, but even if you hit the flanks of these peaks during

OPPOSITE: **British Columbia's mountains offer adventur- ous skiers tough terrain to explore, including high alpine bowls and steep old-growth forests.**

PAGES 206-207: **Snowcats transport skiers to more than 25,000 acres (10,117.2 ha) of backcountry.**

a dry spell, you're likely to get face shots. The company has access to more than 21,500 acres (8,700.7 ha) of terrain, much of it north facing and protected from the elements, and the team of 20 guides has a nose for deep snow.

In a single day, skiers and snowboarders can get eight to 12 runs, racking up as much as 18,000 vertical feet (5,486.4 m). The best of those trails is Sundog, an east-facing run that starts atop a 7,545-foot-high (2,300 m) saddle and descends for almost 2,000 vertical feet. "I think people love it because it has a little bit of everything, from big open powder turns to tree skiing," says Towes.

Starting in the alpine beside a shark-fin rock that stands some 300 feet (91.4 m) tall, you'll look out at the jagged spires of Valhalla Provincial Park before descending a 25- to 35-degree slope. You'll then navigate through well-spaced spruce and balsam fir trees before reaching the awaiting cat, which you'll hop aboard for another run. "This is avalanche terrain, so you need good stability to ski it," says Towes. "When you do, it's a special day."

WHERE TO STAY

The Hume Hotel and Spa in Nelson was opened in 1898, and now, several renovations later, has beautifully decorated rooms and a spa that offers a deep-tissue massage that's sure to work out the kinks that 18,000 vertical feet (5,486.4 m) of skiing might cause. The best part: the Library Lounge, which has a brick fireplace and leather-bound books on the wall and serves delicious cocktails, including a cranberry spice margarita.

MONT-TREMBLANT RESORT

Must-Try Trail: Tunnel

MAX ELEVATION: 2,871 feet (875 m)   **AVERAGE SNOWFALL:** 178 inches (452.1 cm)
SKIABLE TERRAIN: 755 acres (305 ha)   **OPEN SKI SEASON:** November to April

With a village composed of cobblestone streets and brightly painted old-world-style shops and restaurants, Mont-Tremblant is a sort of Epcot Center for skiers and snowboarders. Rue des Remparts, one of the village's streets, for example, is a replica of Rue du Petit-Champlain in Vieux-Québec, and the resort's Saint-Bernard chapel is a replica of the Saint Lawrence parish church on Ile d'Orléans, which was erected just outside Québec City at the end of the 17th century.

Thick with Québécois culture, the resort offers up everything from French-speaking street performances to the region's culinary staple: poutine, which is french fries, cheese curds, and gravy. Theme park–like cultural immersion aside, Tremblant also has some of the better alpine ski and snowboard trails on the east coast.

Ironically, the ski area was founded in 1939 by an American, Joe Ryan, who'd visited the Laurentian Mountains a year earlier, looked out at Mont-Tremblant, at 2,871 feet high one of the tallest peaks in the range, and decided it should become a ski area. In 1939, he constructed one of the first chairlifts in North America (the first was at Idaho's Sun Valley Resort). Today, the ski area has 14 lifts and 102 trails, the majority of them rated as advanced or expert terrain.

OPPOSITE: Skiers and snowboarders make their way down one of 102 trails offered at Mont-Tremblant.

PAGES 210-211: A snowboarder makes his way through the trees on a run down Tunnel.

Among the best of those is Tunnel, so named because the branches of the coniferous and deciduous trees on either side of the run grow out and over the trail, creating a canopy that makes it feel as though you're skiing through a tunnel.

"Skiing down it, it kind of feels like you're way out in the forest, in the middle of nowhere," says Erik Guay, a former member of the Canadian National Ski Team who grew up skiing at Tremblant. "The trees covering it definitely produce a cool effect."

Originally, the narrow swath was cut to make room for a rope tow, which eventually gave way to a platter lift. Over the years, locals would poach the run and ski alongside the lift. But by 2014, the lift was removed, and the 322-vertical-foot trail with an approximately 40-degree pitch was opened to the public. Though it's occasionally groomed, you're most likely to find Tunnel full of bumps or powder. "I like it in the spring, when the snow gets softer and you're skiing slush moguls," says Guay. "It's a leg burner if you ski it top to bottom."

WHERE TO STAY

Mont-Tremblant has over 75 restaurants, a casino, and, with 1,900 lodging units, plenty of places to stay. The biggest and, arguably, the nicest of those options is Fairmont Tremblant. Situated at the base of the mountain (ski-in, ski-out), it has a full-service spa and a culinary brasserie, serving dishes like Québec country lamb cutlets and choux gras.

KITZBÜHEL SKI AREA

Must-Try Trail: The Streif

MAX ELEVATION: 6,562 feet (2,000.1 m)   **AVERAGE SNOWFALL: 150 inches (381 cm)**
SKIABLE TERRAIN: 1,401 acres (567 ha)   **OPEN SKI SEASON: December to April**

E very January, the town of Kitzbühel, Austria, hosts one of the biggest parties in Europe. For an entire weekend, close to 100,000 face-painted, flag-waving revelers descend on the small, medieval village—population about 8,000—in the Tyrolean Alps. Led by oompah bands (composed of deep brass instruments), they march up and down the cobblestone streets past pastel-colored hotels and boutiques, piling into the bars and restaurants where they stuff their faces with schnitzel and chug weissbier. For a few hours, they gather at the base of the Hahnenkamm mountain, a 5,617-foot (1,712.1 m) peak, and cheer on the best ski racers in the world as they compete in the sport's superbowl.

Named for the mountain, the Hahnenkamm ski race was first held in 1931. Since 1937, the competition has been held on the Streif (stripe), a 2,822-vertical-foot (860.2 m) trail that's considered the most technically demanding racecourse in the world. "What separates Kitzbühel from every other race is that it's in your face right from the beginning," says Daron Rahlves, only one of two Americans to win the race. "It's one of the toughest mental challenges of the season, both because of how technical it is and because of what it means: for a downhiller, winning here is bigger than winning at the Olympics."

Before the race, the Streif is injected with water, a technique that turns the

CULTURAL IMMERSION

The beautiful ringing of bells that you hear each day in the town of Kitzbühel at 11 a.m. and 5 p.m. comes from Saint Catherine's Church in the town center, which was built in 1360 and is a perfectly preserved example of the High Gothic period. Its high spire stands out, and the church is considered a landmark.

OPPOSITE: A racer speeds down the Streif Course during a men's downhill competition in 2020.

PAGES 214-215: The Vordestadt in Old Town offers shops, cafés, and restaurants to explore.

snow into fast glare ice, a surface that requires ski edges as sharp as obsidian knives to carve around the tight corners. Just eight seconds into the race, skiers are nuking down the trail at over 60 miles per hour (96.6 km/h) as they enter the Mausefalle (mousetrap), a section of course that launches racers some 200 feet (60.7 m) off a jump and into a compression, a terrain trap that's been known to eat up some of the very best ski racers.

If athletes do make it past the Mausefalle, they'll hit top speeds of around 90 miles per hour (144.8 km/h) and withstand G forces as high as 3.1 (astronauts experience G forces as high as 3 during space shuttle launches), all while navigating many more obstacles: fall-away turns, side hills, and more big jumps, particularly the Hausberg and Zielschuss, both of which send skiers flying. "You cross the finish line and you're thinking, *Hell, yeah, I made it down that thing in one piece,*" says Rahlves.

When the Streif isn't glazed for racing, it's a fun, moderately challenging groomed trail. "I've skied down it in soft snow," says Rahlves. "You need to

WHERE TO STAY

The Tennerhof Gourmet & Spa de Charme Hotel looks like a cuckoo clock. The hotel's rooms are furnished with beds and bureaus decorated with Tyrolean floral designs; a spa—complete with a sauna and pool—offers a menu of various massages; and the restaurant, which serves seven-course meals, is considered the best in Kitzbühel.

ABOVE: **As daylight fades, skiers take the day's last runs down slopes at Hahnenkamm.**

OPPOSITE: **Snowy trees and ski chalets frame the Streif race hill on a snowy day.**

make good turns, but an advanced skier can make it down no problem." The average grade of the piste is a gentle 15 degrees—large sections of the Streif are virtually flat corridors through larch trees—with the steepest, hardest part of the descent, the Mausefalle (when you're not soaring off it at 60 miles per hour/96.6 km/h, you're skiing down its face), being around 60 degrees.

Though elite ski racers make it down the trail in under two minutes, casually skiing or snowboarding the Streif should take between five and 10 minutes, plenty of time to take in views of the Wilder Kaiser Mountains, a band of sheer limestone peaks on the other side of the valley. The trail ends right back in the town of Kitzbühel, which is festive even when the Hahnenkamm isn't taking place. "I take off my skis and go to the Londoner," says Rahlves. "It has a wall of fame—photos of all the guys who've won the race—and it hosts the biggest party in town after the race. It's an institution."

SAINT ANTON AM ARLBERG

Must-Try Trail: North Face of Valluga

MAX ELEVATION: 9,222 feet (2,810.9 m) **AVERAGE SNOWFALL:** 450 inches (1,143 cm)
SKIABLE TERRAIN: 1,102 acres (446 ha) **OPEN SKI SEASON:** December to April

Saint Anton am Arlberg (known simply as Saint Anton), in the Austrian state of Tyrol, is considered the birthplace of modern skiing. It was here, in the 1920s, that Hannes Schneider, a ski instructor, created the Arlberg technique, named for the Arlberg Massif, the mountains that form this section of the Tyrolean Alps. Better known as the stem christie, it's a method of turning skis that involves forming a wedge to initiate the change in direction, followed by bringing the skis parallel to complete the turn. It revolutionized how the sport was taught, and put a spotlight on Saint Anton, causing people to flock to the area to learn how to ski.

The village of Saint Anton, which sprawls through the narrow Stanzertal Valley, is well known for something else: its party scene. After the lifts close, you'll find tourists from all over the world eating, drinking, and dancing at establishments like Bobos—where you can chase chicken wings and pilsners with house music spun by a DJ—almost until the lifts start running again the next morning.

But pace yourself. This part of Austria is also known to have some of the best powder skiing in Europe. That's due to Atlantic storms that blow in from the west, hitting these 8,000 (2,438.4) to 9,000-foot-high (2,743.2 m) mountains and becoming trapped, dumping around 450 inches (1,143 cm) of light, dry snow each season. That snow piles up on five ski areas, all of them

APRÈS SKI

The north face of Valluga will spit you out into the ski area of Zürs. Upon finishing one of Tyrol's classic descents, it's only fitting that you refuel with classic Tyrolean food. You can find that at the Hirlanda, near the base of Zürs, which serves up wiener schnitzel, spaetzle, and kaiserschmarrn.

OPPOSITE: Seemingly by himself, a skier makes his way from the summit of Valluga in the sweeping Austrian Alps.

PAGES 220-221: Skiers enjoy an après-ski drink at the Icebar Lech.

connected under the banner of Ski Arlberg, forming a network of more than 185 miles (297.7 km) of trails that are accessed by nearly 100 cable cars and lifts. But the best skiing in the region, an approximately 8,000-foot (2,438.4 m) descent from the top of Valluga—at 9,215 feet (2,808.7 m) the highest mountain in the Arlberg region—isn't part of the ski resort, and to ski down it, you must hire a local guide.

Guides are regularly available to help skiers and snowboarders make their way down the north face of Valluga, many of whom have International Federation of Mountain Guides Association (IFMGA) certifications, which require advanced training in rock climbing and back-country safety.

To access Valluga, you ride two aerial trams (Vallugabahn 1 and 2). "The trams are there for sightseeing," says Angelika Kaufmann, a local ski guide. "But you can access the skiing by using them."

Before you ski down Valluga, you'll want to take some time to be a sightseer yourself. In the

WHERE TO STAY

Ullr, a Norse god, is considered the patron saint of skiing, so it's appropriate that Saint Anton's newest hotel, Ullrhaus, pays homage to him. Right in downtown Saint Anton, the hotel's modern, minimalist design features a common area with a fireplace and bar as well as a spa with an indoor pool and a Finnish sauna.

ABOVE: Saint Anton's pedestrian center offers plenty of hotels, restaurants, and shops to enjoy.

OPPOSITE: A gondola transports skiers past snow-covered pines to powder-covered slopes.

foreground, craggy, knife-edge ridgelines look like the serpentine backs of dragons. Farther away, several prominent peaks are visible, including Glärnisch, a 9,560-foot (2,913.9 m) mountain in Switzerland.

The initial descent down the north face of Valluga is the most difficult part of the trail. After crossing a bridge, you're forced to scramble down rocks in your ski boots (wear a backpack that you can strap your skis to) while holding a fixed line. From here, you'll ski a tight, steep, approximately 650-foot (200 m) couloir. (Keep an eye out for ibex, a type of mountain goat that sometimes roams this section of the mountain.)

"Once you get through that, the trail is all open bowls that often have great light powder," says Kaufmann. "It's rolling slopes through the valley, like skiing on a big open sea of white all the way down."

VAL D'ISÈRE SKI RESORT

Must-Try Trail: La Face de Bellevarde

MAX ELEVATION: 11,339 feet (3,456.1 m) **AVERAGE SNOWFALL:** 207 inches (525.8 cm)
SKIABLE TERRAIN: 2,471 acres (1,000 ha) **OPEN SKI SEASON:** November to May

Growing up in Val d'Isère, Jean-Claude Killy knew that the face of Bellevarde, a 9,274-foot (2,826.7 m) peak that rose up from the town, would make for a great downhill racecourse. Killy, who would go on to win three gold medals at the 1968 Winter Olympics and earn a reputation as one of the greatest ski racers of all time, was named co-president of the 1992 Winter Olympics in Albertville, France. And the alpine racing events were to be held at Val-d'Isère, a ski area and village in southeastern France that manages to be both chic and traditional (five-star hotels and spas blend seamlessly with stone-roofed chalets and farmhouse restaurants).

Killy was in charge of overseeing course design, and he hired former Olympic champion Bernhard Russi to build a world-class downhill track on Bellevarde. The result: a course that sent racers hurtling down the mountain at an average speed of nearly 62 miles per hour (98.2 km/h), flying hundreds of feet in the air off jumps (Austria's Patrick Ortlieb won the race).

La Face is considered one of the best trails in the Alps for advanced and expert skiers and snowboarders—particularly those who love carving into freshly groomed snow and making high-speed arcs through corduroy. East facing, La Face is lit up by the sun in the morning, making it the ideal time to rip down the 1,831-vertical-foot (558.1 m), steep, twisty trail, taking time only to stop and admire the jagged, snow-caked Alps on the horizon.

WHERE TO STAY

At 8,369 feet (2,550.9 m), Refuge de Solaise is the highest hotel in France. The guest rooms' barnwood siding, plush beds, and tiled bathrooms make for comfortable crash pads, and the wellness center with skier-specific massages, an indoor heated pool, and a hot tub that looks out at the valley below is a one-stop recovery shop for tired muscles.

An off-piste skier tackles tough terrain in the mountains of Val d'Isère.

ALPE D'HUEZ SKI AREA

Must-Try Trail: La Sarenne

MAX ELEVATION: 10,925 feet (3,330 m)   **AVERAGE SNOWFALL: 122 inches (309.9 cm)**
SKIABLE TERRAIN: 2,020 acres (817.5 ha)   **OPEN SKI SEASON: December to April**

La Sarenne, a 9.9-mile (16 km) descent in the French Alps, is the longest black diamond run in Europe. And although it has an expert rating, intermediate skiers and snowboarders can easily tackle the trail's mostly moderate pitch, almost all of which is groomed. In fact, since La Sarenne is as much a scenic tour of the region—massifs and snow-caked pyramidal peaks loom in the near distance—as it is a ski run, intermediates might actually appreciate the slower pace that allows more time to take in the impressive views.

The tour begins at the top of Pic Blanc, at 9,940 feet (3,330 m) the highest elevation at the ski area. From here, Mont Blanc, the highest peak in the Alps, dominates the skyline to the north. Also prominent are the Needles, a row of pointy spires that will accompany you most of the way down the trail. Descending from the top is the most difficult part of La Sarenne: a 985-foot-long (300 m), 28-degree pitch typically bumped up with moguls. But once you've made it through the gauntlet, the trail is buffed out and mellower.

Along the way, you can stop at picnic tables that line the trail, keeping an eye out for chamois, a native goat-antelope. As you make your way down the final couple of miles, you'll ski through the deep valley of Gorges de Sarenne, past a gurgling brook, before reaching Auberge de la Combe Haute, a hut where you can celebrate with red wine and charcuterie before pushing on a little bit farther to the Chalvet chairlift and back to Alpe d'Huez's village.

WHERE TO STAY

If it wasn't located slope-side, thus making it hard to ignore the skiing outside your window, you might spend all your time inside Hotel Au Chamois d'Or. The comfy rooms are bathed in blond wood and linen, leather stools surround the bar where top-shelf booze flows, the fireplace is always well stoked, and the spa has numerous offerings.

From the Sarenne glacier ski top terrain and enjoy views of the French Alps.

GARMISCH-CLASSIC

Must-Try Trail: Kandahar

MAX ELEVATION: 6,726 feet (2,050.1 m)   **AVERAGE SNOWFALL: 340 inches (863.6 cm)**
SKIABLE TERRAIN: 25 miles (40 km)   **OPEN SKI SEASON: December to March**

When Steven Nyman arrives in Garmisch-Partenkirchen, Germany, each winter, he feels at home. "There's a U.S. Army garrison right down the road, so there's a strong American vibe," says Nyman, a member of the U.S. Alpine Ski Team. "The town is full of American bars and American military guys driving big American-made trucks. Except for the Bavarian chalets and weisswurst, there are times when you think you could be in Colorado or Utah."

Rising up above Garmisch-Partenkirchen is Garmisch-Classic, a ski area with 25 miles (40 km) of trails. Kandahar, a long, steep trail that hosted ski racing at the 1936 Olympics, was the track used for downhill and super-G events at the 2011 World Alpine Ski Championship. Each year the trail is home to men's and women's World Cup downhills and is considered one of the most challenging groomed runs in Europe. "It's north-facing, bumpy, and icy," says Nyman. "Even when you're not racing down the trail, you still have to be on top of it and making good turns to get to the bottom in one piece."

The trail starts atop Kreuzjoch, a 5,640-foot (1,719.1 m) peak, descending a thigh-burning 2,362 vertical feet (719.9 m) down a wide slope with evergreens on either side. "You go around sweeping turns," says Nyman, "down pitches that feel like they're about 60 degrees, and through a ravine-like feature that's dark and steep—all the way to the base of the ski area."

WHERE TO EAT

Despite the American influence (there are several restaurants that claim to have the "best burger in town"), there are still places like Gasthof Fraundorfer, which delivers the look and feel of a classic Bavarian eatery—wait staff are dressed in dirndls—and serves favorites such as potato soup, goulash, and crispy pork knuckle alongside lagers and weissbier.

Challenging and steep, the Kandahar downhill run is one of Garmisch-Partenkirchen's top trails.

PSILORITIS (MOUNT IDA)

Must-Try Trail: North Face

MAX ELEVATION: 8,058 feet (2,456.1 m)   **AVERAGE SNOWFALL:** 160 inches (406.4 cm)
SKIABLE TERRAIN: 10,000 acres (4,046.9 ha)   **OPEN SKI SEASON:** January to April

Psiloritis, a mountain on the Greek island of Crete, is revered in the annals of Greek mythology. It was here that Zeus, the god of the sky, lightning, and thunder, was hidden in a cave from his father, Cronus, the ruler of the Titans. According to the legend, Cronus had been given a prophecy that one day, his children would overthrow him and so, to protect his reign, he swallowed each child at birth. Zeus, however, survived on Psiloritis (also known as Mount Ida). Later, he tricked Cronus into vomiting out his siblings, and together they successfully overthrew their father.

More recently, the mountain has become revered for another reason: Backcountry skiers and snowboarders have discovered that Psiloritis's 30- to 40-degree, wide-open, treeless flanks, which look out onto the turquoise waters of the Libyan Sea to the south and the Aegean Sea to the north, make for some of the best turns in Europe. "Foreigners have been coming to Greece to ski tour for years, but the numbers have always been small," says Constantine Papanicolaou, the director of Frozen Ambrosia, a production company that's made several films about skiing in Greece. "Overall, the image of summer in the Greek islands was so pervasive that the winter season was eclipsed entirely." That despite the fact that Psiloritis, which tops out at 8,058 feet (2,456.1 m), benefits from cold air that blows in from the north and mixes with maritime storms, producing heavy snowfall throughout the winter.

CULTURAL IMMERSION

Just an hour-and-a-half drive from Psiloritis is Knossos, a 4,000-year-old archaeological site. Touring through Knossos gives you a fascinating look at ancient frescos and Minoan columns, as well as irrigation drains, terracotta pipes, water tanks, and cisterns for drinking water.

OPPOSITE: Skiers prep their gear outside the Katsivelli Refuge in the White Mountains of Crete.

PAGES 232-233: The Psiloritis mountain range gets plenty of skier-friendly snow cover.

In 2014, a small group of skiers began taking full advantage of those snowy winters and started hosting a ski mountaineering race, an event in which hundreds of competitors skin to the top of Psiloritis, then descend the mountain as fast as they can (first one to the bottom wins). The race changed local perceptions of the mountain. "The people who live in Livadia, one of the villages at the base of the north side of the mountain, are mostly shepherds," says Papanicolaou. "In the summer, they'd bring the sheep up into the mountains, but they feared the mountains in the winter. If you went up there and got stuck, you could die." But the race showed the villagers that they could venture up Psiloritis in the winter and have fun skiing down it. Since the race began, a local opened a ski shop and the village's priest and the president of the local community regularly ski the mountain.

To join them, it's best to hire a foreign guide who has been certified by the Union Internationale des Associations de Guides de Montagnes (there are no locally certified guides). In the

WHERE TO EAT

About 19 miles (30.6 km) from Psiloritis is Peskesi, a restaurant in Heraklion that's tucked away in a side alley inside a restored Byzantine-era mansion. The local favorite, near the shores of the Aegean Sea, serves recipes dating back to ancient Cretan times, including *foukaki* (a sort of pork pie), *kreokakavos* (pork roasted with honey and thyme), and croquettes filled with various vegetables.

ABOVE: A ski tourer drops gear during a break at the Kallergi Hut refuge.

OPPOSITE: A skier gazes out at the snow-covered mountains of Crete before dropping in from a ridge.

springtime, when the sun bakes the snow into a smooth surface of granular corn snow—"It's some of the best corn you'll find anywhere," says Papanicolaou—begin skinning up the north face of Psiloritis from the Migero Plateau, 5,183 feet (1,579.8 m) up the mountain (a road takes you past the village of Livadia to the plateau). After three to four hours of skinning, you'll reach the peak, where a small Greek Orthodox church stands. From here, you'll make three or four low-angle turns off the top, before rolling onto a sustained 35-degree pitch that descends for over 3,000 vertical feet (914.4 m) back down to the road.

"What strikes me the most about ski touring in Greece and Crete is how big the terrain is and how easy it is to access," says Papanicolaou. "Anywhere else, these mountains would be covered with hotels and chalets. Instead, they're completely pristine."

LONGHORN MOUNTAIN

Must-Try Trail: Whale's Mouth

MAX ELEVATION: 6,921 feet (2,109 m)   **AVERAGE SNOWFALL: Unknown**
SKIABLE TERRAIN: Unknown   **OPEN SKI SEASON: Variable**

In mountains throughout the world, just before sunrise and right after sunset, snow-capped peaks become awash in warm hues of red, pink, and purple. Known as alpenglow (derived from the German word for "Alp glow"), most skiers and snowboarders realize that the phenomenon is a fleeting spectacle. But during springtime in Iceland, the sun hovers low for hours, long enough to enjoy a ski descent from summit to sea while immersed in the magic light. "It's otherworldly," says former U.S. Ski Team member Keely Kelleher, founder of Keely's Camps for Girls, which hosts women's backcountry ski trips in Iceland. "You think, Where am I? and start to believe it's the land of elves and trolls and fairies."

Coinciding with Iceland's light show is the country's corn snow season, a coveted surface consistency that in most parts of the world is highly dependent on timing: hit the slopes too early and the snow is rock-hard; too late and it's sticky slush. But in Iceland, the corn snow remains an ideal granular consistency from sunup to sundown. "Its perfection has something to do with the moisture content of the snow and the latitude," says Kelleher. "It's this surfy, bottomless, hero corn I've never found anywhere else in the world."

The bucket list way to access this prime corn snow is by sailboat. Several outfitters in the town of Ísafjörður, a traditional fishing village in northwest Iceland, lead sail-to-ski trips to Hornstrandir Nature Reserve, an area rife with

OPPOSITE: Originally built as a home in 1923, Kviar Lodge now serves as a base for skiing, hiking, and wildlife viewing in the Hornstrandir Nature Reserve.

PAGES 238-239: Hornstrandir, devoid of human residents since the 1950s, offers spectacular skiing and views of surrounding fjords.

ski-touring terrain. Aboard what's akin to a floating backcountry hut, you'll sail from fjord to fjord each night. And during the day, you'll load onto Zodiacs—rigid inflatable boats—that take you ashore, allowing you to skin up and ski down everything from wide-open faces and bowls to steep couloirs.

"Most runs in Hornstrandir aren't named—it's not the Iceland way," says Kelleher. That said, Kelleher's group of female guides and skiers did christen her favorite run: "Whale's Mouth," a 3,000-vertical-foot (914.4 m) line on the southwest face of Longhorn Mountain. "You ski over this hump and all the way to the shoreline," says Kelleher. "It feels like you're skiing into a whale's mouth."

To get to Whale's Mouth, you'll sail three hours from Ísafjörður up the Veid Fjord. After that, the trek up to the peak takes several more hours. But there's a massive payoff: From the dramatic convex summit, you'll look out over a vast treeless wilderness of contrasting white peaks and black ocean before easing into a 45-degree rollover that settles into a wide-open 30-degree run, which, timed correctly, is bathed in alpenglow.

OFF THE SLOPES

A volcanic island straddling two diverging tectonic plates, Iceland bubbles with geothermal activity. No ski trip to Iceland is complete without a dip in one of the country's hundreds of hot springs or *sundlaugs*, massive public pools, some of them lined with lava stone, that are said to improve well-being: Iceland's soaking culture has been linked to its consistent high ranking in the World Happiness Report.

ALTA BADIA

Must-Try Trail: Gran Risa

MAX ELEVATION: 9,114 feet (2,777.9 m)   **AVERAGE SNOWFALL:** 103 inches (261.6 cm)
SKIABLE TERRAIN: 80.8 miles (130 km)   **OPEN SKI SEASON:** December to April

One of Alta Badia ski area's most famous slopes was created at the end of the nineteenth century, some 30 years before the ski area officially existed. Residents of the northern Italian town of La Villa, tucked into the Badia Valley at the base of the Dolomites, harvested the mountain's pine and larch for building material and to heat their homes during the cold winter. To haul the fallen timber down the mountain, the loggers created a pathway, the Gran Risa, which translates to "the great split." In the process, the loggers unknowingly created a trail so long and steep that it is now one of the most popular places for the World Cup ski racing tour. Of course, you don't have to go fast to enjoy Gran Risa. Most people prefer to hit the always groomed north-facing trail in the morning, when they can carve their edges through firm streaks of fresh corduroy.

Getting to the trail is simple: From La Villa, you ride the Piz La Ila cable car to 7,296 feet (2,223.8 m). Upon exiting the lift, you have 360-degree views of the Dolomites. The trail is about 650 feet (198.1 m) from the top of the lift and quickly becomes narrow and steep, reaching angles of 53 degrees. Mercifully, the leg-burning, 4,117-foot (1,254.9 m) descent finishes right back in La Villa, where you can rest and refuel with local Ladin cuisine, including *kaiserschmarrn,* a chopped-up sweet omelet filled with fruit and served with jam and sugar and a favorite of ski racing great Lindsey Vonn.

APRÈS SKI

Alta Badia is famous for its gourmet food, including the cuisine served at some 50 mountain huts spread out around the mountain. Of those, the Rifugio Ütia de Bioch, located in the center of the ski area, is a can't miss. The hut has a large, sunny terrace; a bar; a large wine cellar; and a restaurant serving Ladin and Tyrolean favorites like speck, pork ribs, and strudel.

Set in the Dolomites, Alta Badia is encircled by imposing rock faces and rugged ridges.

ÅRE SKI AREA

Must-Try Trail: Baksidan

MAX ELEVATION: 4,659 feet (1,420 m)   **AVERAGE SNOWFALL:** 153 inches (388 cm)
SKIABLE TERRAIN: 790.7 acres (319.9 ha)   **OPEN SKI SEASON:** December to May

Locals call it cauliflower: puffy formations of rime ice that famously stick to everything at Sweden's Åre Ski Area—trees, rocks, buildings, chairlifts, gondolas, and trails—making it look as though the entire resort has been spray-coated with the pale, bushy vegetable. The impressive accretion of ice creates an otherworldly landscape, but it also begets tough skiing and snowboarding conditions. Making turns on rime ice down any of the ski area's 105 trails—ranging from kids' runs that have bridges and tunnels, to world-famous terrain parks that breed X Games champions, to long, steep groomers that host World Cup slalom races each year—feels like skiing on marbles.

That's why skiers and snowboarders in the know head off the backside of the ski area's 4,659-foot (1,420 m) peak to ski Baksidan (it literally translates to "backside"), a wide, treeless backcountry trail. Because it's not skied nearly as much as the runs inside the ski area's boundaries, it often has a nice layer of powder snow covering the rime ice. "You can ski it a day or two after a storm and still find fresh tracks," says Janne Tjärnström, a ski coach at the ski area.

To get to Baksidan, you ride the tram from the base of the ski area to a docking station near the peak of the mountain. From there, you can hike 20 minutes on a groomed cat road or hitch a snowmobile ride 600 feet to the top of Åreskutan, where you'll find Toppstugan, Sweden's highest café. Founded in 1892, 17 years before the ski area opened, the café serves up

OPPOSITE: With some trails topping out at 4,100 feet (1,249.7 m) at Åre Ski Area, you'll find yourself skiing above the clouds.

PAGES 244-245: Åre is one of the largest and best-known ski areas in Scandinavia, with 40 ski lifts and 103 runs.

classic Swedish treats, such as homemade waffles with cloudberry jam, alongside 360-degree views of endless boreal forest; the village of Åre, with its red farmhouses and world-class restaurants (where you can still dine on reindeer and lingonberries); and skaters gliding across Åresjön, a 2.5-mile-long (4.02 km) frozen lake right at the base of the mountain.

From Toppstugan, you traverse beyond the ski area boundary and access Backsidan (because this is backcountry terrain, you should carry avalanche equipment and consider hiring a local guide). Åre's multitude of Freeride World Tour champions, such as Reine Barkered, Kristofer Turdell, and Carl Regnér, might choose to drop into the Banana, a steep, 15-foot-wide (4.6 m) chute. But Tjärnström prefers the northeast-facing line that's littered with rime-ice-covered rocks, which, coated in powder, transform into pillowy formations that he can pop off. "This face of Backsidan is a short ski," he says. "But it's super steep—45 to 50 degrees—and the snow is always good."

ALTERNATIVE ROUTE

If you don't want to drop into the backcountry, you can ski Störtloppet, a scenic trail that winds its way 1,500 vertical feet (457.2 m) down Åre and hosts World Cup and World Championship downhill races. Two legendary downhill champions, Lindsey Vonn and Norwegian overall World Cup and Olympic champion Aksel Svindal, finished their illustrious careers on this trail. Ski it at the end of the day, says Tjärnström, and you'll feel as though you're skiing into the sunset.

TITLIS ENGELBERG

Must-Try Trail: Laub

MAX ELEVATION: 10,623 feet (3,237.9 m)   **AVERAGE SNOWFALL: 118.1 inches (300 cm)**
SKIABLE TERRAIN: 82 acres (33.2 ha)   **OPEN SKI SEASON: October to May**

t's hard to imagine a more perfect powder run than Laub: a wide-open, 40-degree, fall-line ramp that descends for a remarkable 4,000 vertical feet (1,219.2 m)—a longer vertical drop than most North American ski areas—and, thanks to frequent storms that hover over central Switzerland's Uri Alps, often serves up skiers and snowboarders with waist-deep turns. "I had the best run of my life down Laub," says Marcus Caston, a professional skier from Utah who floated down the slope after an overnight storm dropped 3 feet (0.9 m) of snow on the surrounding mountains. "I was experiencing all the positive feelings of powder skiing; then I realized that that elation wasn't stopping. It was just going on and on, like a dream."

Caston is far from the only pro skier to heap praise on Laub. "It doesn't have rocks and trees, so you can make autopilot giant slalom turns without ever breaking your rhythm, looking out at views of Lake Lucerne in between face shots," says Sven Brunso, whom SKI magazine called the most photographed skier in history. "It's the ultimate powder skier's heaven."

Laub is located on the north-facing flank of Titlis, a pointy, 10,623-foot (3,237.9 m) limestone peak that rises above Engelberg, Switzerland, a medieval town that's best known for three things: a Benedictine monastery that was constructed in 1120 (it's worth a visit), a cheese factory that produces

OPPOSITE: With more than 40 miles (64.4 km) of runs, Engelberg's slopes of all difficulties await skiers.

PAGES 248-249: The Titlis Cliff Walk suspension bridge hangs 9,842.5 feet (3,000 m) above sea level.

Engelberger Klosterglocke (a mild cheese molded into the shape of the monastery's bell), and a base camp for some of the best off-piste skiing in all of Europe.

Skiers began exploring Titlis in the early 1900s and over the years developed what's known as the Big 5: five trails that consist of crevassed glaciers, precipitous couloirs, and frightening exposure. Of the five, Laub isn't only the most beloved; its consistent, mostly inconsequential terrain also makes it the most accessible, so advanced intermediates can easily tackle the slope.

To get to the trail, you take several lifts from the base of Titlis, eventually riding the Laubersgrat chairlift to the midway point of the mountain. From there, you'll traverse across a ridge and then drop into the run. After making several hundred turns down the face of Laub, you'll end up at Gasthaus Gerschnialp, a small hotel with a restaurant that serves classic Swiss dishes, including raclette, as well as älplermagronen, an alpine version of macaroni and cheese with caramelized onion, Gruyère, and warm applesauce.

WHERE TO STAY

Less than 400 feet (121.9 m) from the train station is Ski Lodge Engelberg. Its bubbly staff greets young skiers and snowboarders from around the world with cozy, well-designed rooms (think: flannel sheets, vintage ski posters, and white tile bathrooms), a renowned brasserie, and a lively bar—the meeting spot in town—filled with soon-to-be ski partners.

VERBIER SKI AREA

Must-Try Trail: Tortin

MAX ELEVATION: 10,025 feet (3,329.9 m) **AVERAGE SNOWFALL:** 331 inches (840.7 cm)
SKIABLE TERRAIN: 400 acres (161.9 ha) **OPEN SKI SEASON:** November to May

Because it's never groomed, because it's a steep 35- to 40-degree pitch, and because it's a long 2,277-vertical-foot (694 m) descent, Tortin (also known as Chassoure) is considered one of the most challenging trails in Europe. "It's such a famous run that tourists come here to ski it so they can go home and tell their friends that they skied Tortin," says Anna Smoothy, a former pro skier who now works as head of marketing for Faction Skis, a company based in Verbier, Switzerland. "As you're riding up the Col de Chassoure gondola, a nice eight-minute ride that gets you to the top of the trail, you see them navigating their way through waist-high moguls. It can be pretty entertaining."

Tortin is part of a 256-mile (412 km) network of trails at Les Quatre Vallées, the largest ski area in Switzerland. Best known for the village of Verbier—a mixture of fur-coat-wearing bankers and oil barons who stay at chic hotels and ski bums clad in faded parkas who party late into the night at more than a dozen pubs and nightclubs—Les Quatre Vallées trails range from easy groomers to off-piste trails full of deep powder. Since Tortin is northeast facing, the typically bumped-up, football-field-wide slope is rarely touched by the sun. "The snow in the whole Tortin zone stays cold," says Smoothy, "so you get this hard-pack, chalky snow that's really fast and fun."

APRÈS SKI

Verbier has a number of five-star restaurants, but a local favorite for food isn't in Verbier and it's not what you might expect at a ritzy Swiss resort. Le Tipi is, in fact, a teepee located at 6,561 feet (1,999.8 m) in Veysonnaz, one of the small villages surrounding the Les Quatre Vallées. According to Smoothy, it has "delicious crepes, ice cream, and coffee."

Dusk settles over the picturesque Verbier village on a clear winter evening.

OUKAÏMEDEN SKI RESORT

Must-Try Trail: Grande Combe

MAX ELEVATION: 10,702 feet (3,262 m)   **AVERAGE SNOWFALL:** 40 inches (101.6 cm)
SKIABLE TERRAIN: 6.2 miles (10 km)   **OPEN SKI SEASON:** January to March

When France began its protectorate over a large portion of Morocco in 1912, they infused a bit of French culture into the North African country, including its language, architecture, and fashion—as well as the sport of skiing. "They looked up and saw the potential and beauty of the Atlas Mountains," says Kristoffer Erickson, a ski guide and owner of Atlas Cultural Adventures, a company that takes people on various trips throughout Morocco. "It was only natural that they were drawn to ski them."

Started by French colonialists in the 1930s, Oukaïmeden, with an elevation of 10,702 feet (3,262 m), is Africa's highest ski area (there are only a few on the continent). Just 48 miles (77.2 km) south of Marrakesh, it's also one of the more accessible ski slopes "It's low-hanging fruit," says Erickson. "You leave the desert and palm trees of Marrakesh, drive up a twisty road that's full of switchbacks, and 90 minutes later, you're at the base of the mountain."

Upon arrival, locals are likely to swarm your car, trying to sell you food, mint tea, or a variety of other goods and services, including an impressive array of outdated rental equipment. Though there's a small village about a half mile (0.8 km) from the base of the mountain consisting of a few hotels and restaurants, all you'll find on the slopes are some surface lifts and one double chairlift that sees very little action.

OPPOSITE: A skier uses a rocky cliff ledge as a jump at Oukäimeden ski resort.

PAGES 254-255: At an altitude of 10,498.7 feet (3,200 m), there are stunning views of Morocco from the ski resort's peaks.

"Most visitors are Moroccans who drive up for the day to get a taste of winter conditions and are content to ride the surface lifts on the lower mountain," says Erickson. "You basically have the whole upper mountain to yourself."

The best descent from the top of the ski area is Grand Combe, a smooth bowl on the otherwise craggy mountain. From the top of the trail are views of the plains of Marrakesh to the north and the high peaks of the Atlas Mountains to the south, including Toubkal, which at 13,671 feet (4,166.9 m) is the highest mountain in the range and the highest peak in North Africa. Looking down the trail, you're likely to find a slope that hasn't received fresh snow in several weeks.

But when a storm does roll in, it can dump for several days, transforming Grand Combe into a hell of a powder run: a 30-degree, 2,000-vertical-foot-long (609.6 m), wide-open trail that never gets tracked out. "When that happens, you're making fresh turns all day," says Erickson. "Since it's north facing and nobody else is out skiing, you can still be skiing powder a week after a storm."

WHERE TO STAY

Because Oukaïmeden's lodging options leave much to be desired, you're better off staying in Marrakesh, where you can shell out big money for a room at Royal Mansour Marrakech, a palace-like hotel with indoor gardens and a 26,900-square-foot (2,499.1 sq m) spa. Or you can opt for a more authentic experience at any number of hotels in the Medina section of the city, where you might see a snake charmer outside your hotel.

LAS LEÑAS SKI RESORT

Must-Try Trail: Eduardo Couloir

MAX ELEVATION: 11,253 feet (3,430 m)   **AVERAGE SNOWFALL:** 236 inches (599.4 cm)
SKIABLE TERRAIN: 40,000 acres (16,187.4 ha)   **OPEN SKI SEASON:** June to October

There are a few lifts in the world that are as famous as any trail at any ski area: the KT-22 Express at Squaw Valley, the Jackson Hole Tram, the Vallée Blanche Cable Car that takes you to the summit of Aiguille du Midi, and the Marte, the pride—and occasionally the shame—of Las Leñas, one of the most popular ski resorts in South America. The slow double-chair is renowned for the scope and quality of terrain that it accesses: almost 4,000 vertical feet (1,219.2 m) of above-tree-line skiing and snowboarding on more than 40,000 acres (16,187.4 ha) of runs and hike-to slopes. Many loyal Marte fans liken the chairlift to a heli-ski drop—and its operation is just as fickle. Topping out at 11,253 feet (3,430 m), the Marte is exposed to the full fury of the Andes, including high winds, low visibility, and high avalanche danger, all of which can shut down the lift for an extended period of time. In the 2006 season, for example, the Marte didn't open for a month.

But when it is spinning, you'll push off it and find some of the finest couloir skiing in the world. Accessible from the top of the long ridgeline are some 40 skiable chutes (to avoid skiing one that dead ends in a cliff, hire a guide), but none more famous than Eduardo Couloir, a descent named for ski instructor Eduardo Gutierrez, who lost his life on the trail in 1986. "Easy access and consistent steepness make Eduardo's an iconic run at Las Leñas," says Thomas

OPPOSITE: Skiers are dwarfed by mammoth stone spires at Las Leñas.

PAGES 258-259: To get to prime skiing and backcountry terrain, skiers hike a windy ridge.

Perren, a Swiss instructor and guide who discovered the ski area in the late '80s and spent close to 20 winters skiing its labyrinth of runs. Score Eduardo in ideal conditions—say, after a Santa Rosa storm (when warm spring winds collide with Antarctic cold fronts in late August and early September)—and it's as good as it gets: waist-deep powder turns down a 40- to 45-degree pitch that drops for 3,000 vertical feet (914.4 m).

To begin your journey to Eduardo, you'll ride up the Venus and Neptuno lifts (Marte is Spanish for Mars), two rides that can feel as slow as interplanetary travel. About 40 minutes later, you'll arrive at the Marte lift, which ascends another 20 minutes to the flat-topped summit of Cerro Fosiles.

From there, you'll ski southeast to the Eduardo face—the location of Las Leñas' big-mountain ski competitions. Rocky walls mark the dramatic entrance of Eduardo, an east-facing couloir. "To enter it, you need courage and experience skiing steep terrain," says Perren. "But if you have the ability, it will be a run you'll always remember."

OFF THE SLOPES

Las Leñas is famous for its late night party scene. Most people end up at UFO Point, which is at its wildest from midnight until 4 a.m., pumping electronic music and pouring Argentina's favorite cocktail: Fernet con Coca, a bitter, sweet, medicinal mix of Fernet-Branca with Coca-Cola over ice. If you stay out so late that you miss first chair the next morning, *no hay problema*; the lifts stay open until 5 p.m.

LA PARVA SKI RESORT

Must-Try Trail: La Chimenea

MAX ELEVATION: 11,909.5 feet (3,630 m) **AVERAGE SNOWFALL:** 118 inches (299.7 cm)
SKIABLE TERRAIN: 800 acres (323.8 ha) **OPEN SKI SEASON:** June to September

You're not going to find one of South America's most famous runs on a trail map—but you can get to it via one of Chile's more popular ski areas. Opened in 1953, La Parva, located high above the tree line, has 15 lifts that access 48 named trails inside the ski area boundaries. But some of the best trails are just outside La Parva's gates, including La Chimenea, an approximately 500-vertical foot (152.4 m) chute that looks like a chimney and is renowned for its consistent pitch and impressive views of the Andes. "It's not some crazy Chamonix line that only experts can go down," says Jeremy Jones, a professional snowboarder and owner of Jones Snowboard Company. "If you're an advanced skier or snowboarder, you'll love it."

To get to La Chimenea, you ride the Las Águilas chairlift to 11,482 feet (3,499.7 m), then exit the ski area boundary (be sure to carry avalanche safety equipment; guides are available). The hike to La Chimenea takes a little over an hour, but often, fresh powder turns through the gully make the trek well worth it. "It seems to be a magnet for snow," says Jones. "I've been there on low-snow years, and there always seems to be three times the amount of snow in La Chimenea as anyplace else." The chute exits onto rolling, open terrain that takes you back toward the ski area. "Try to ride La Chimenea in the afternoon, right around sunset," says Jones. "As you ski home, you're so high up that you're looking down on this fluorescent orange that fades to yellow."

APRÈS SKI

Right at the base of the ski area, El Montañes (the mountaineers) serves Chilean wines and local beers alongside pizza and tapas, including burgers and nachos and foods you're less likely to find on an après menu, such as octopus, ceviche, and barbecue ribs.

A skier takes to the air, suspended above the valley of Santiago.

SKI GULMARG

Must-Try Trail: Hapat Khued Bowl

MAX ELEVATION: 13,858 feet (4,224 m)   **AVERAGE SNOWFALL: 550 inches (1,397 cm)**
SKIABLE TERRAIN: 3.2 acres (1.3 ha)   **OPEN SKI SEASON: December to March**

High in the Himalaya, in the northern Indian region of Kashmir, is one of the few ski areas in the world that's located squarely inside a conflict zone. Religious and territorial strife among India, Pakistan, and Kashmiri separatists has existed here since the 1940s, and there's a clear military presence. See for yourself by riding the gondola to the top of Ski Gulmarg—at almost 14,000 feet (4,267.2 m), the second highest ski area in the world after Jade Dragon Snow Mountain in China—to see the faraway peak of K2 (the second highest mountain in the world) and close-up views of Pakistani troops patrolling the Line of Control (the military-patrolled border between Pakistan and India) just beyond the ski area's boundary.

"But the military presence doesn't detract from the experience," says KC Deane, a professional skier who's spent time filming a ski movie at Gulmarg. "It's a bizarre, mind-blowing place. One of the coolest ski experiences in the world." Established in 1927, Gulmarg was originally a summer destination for wealthy tourists looking to escape the heat among vast fields of daisies, forget-me-nots, and buttercups (Gulmarg translates to "meadow of flowers"). Despite regular winter storms that can blow in and drop up to 6 feet (1.8 m) of snow (the ski area averages 550 inches/1,397 cm of snowfall each year), it wasn't until the late 1990s and early 2000s, when two gondolas were built, that Gulmarg really began establishing itself as a ski resort.

APRÈS SKI

With green roofs and tree-bark siding, the Hotel Highlands Park stands out. The hotel has hosted presidents, prime ministers, and Bollywood stars, but it's best known for its restaurant, which serves traditional dishes, including various curries and lamb meatballs.

OPPOSITE: The Khyber Himalayan Resort and Spa in Gulmarg offers skiers an opportunity to relax in serenity.

PAGES 264-265: Gulmarg is suited to advanced and expert skiers who are looking for fresh powder and backcountry terrain.

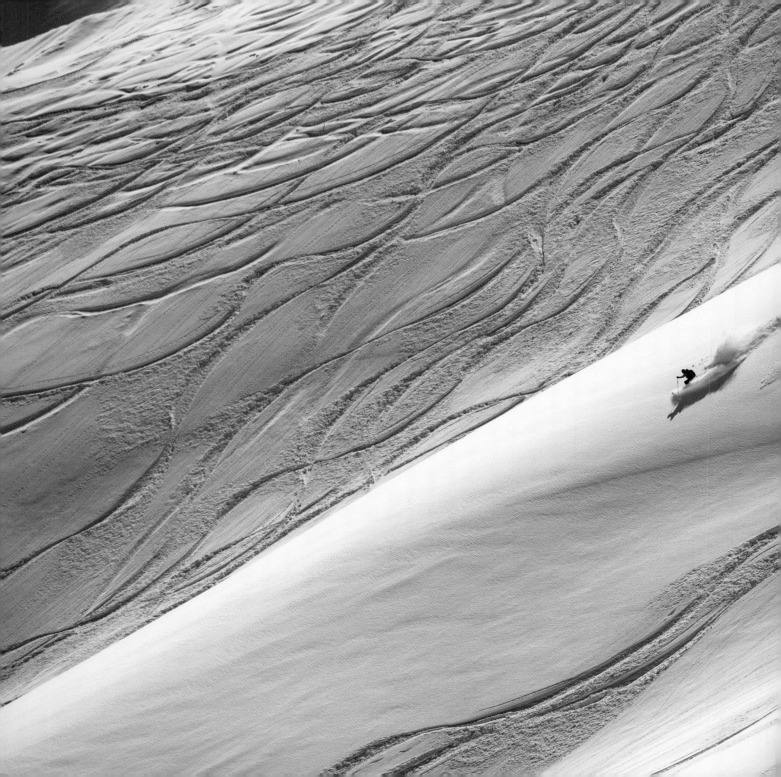

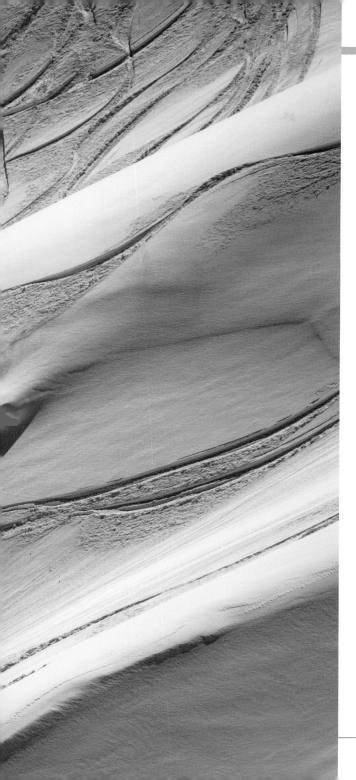

Gulmarg, however, is still not a ski resort in the traditional sense. At the base of the first gondola, men sell chocolate, cigarettes, and tea from wooden boxes that they wear strapped to their bodies. There are no après bars in the dry city, and very few people actually ski or snowboard. Most local visitors are content to sled around on the hills surrounding the base of the mountain. Those who do buy a lift ticket—which only costs $25—ascend the resort's two gondolas to find an unusual layout.

Once atop Apharwat Peak, the mountain on which Ski Gulmarg operates, skiers and snowboarders can go right or left, hiking and sliding along a nearly 5-mile-long (8 km) ridgeline, dropping into wide-open bowls at any moment they see terrain that looks appealing. While everything is open and accessible, only the Gondola Bowl—the 3-acre (1.2 ha) plot right under the two gondolas—is avalanche controlled. Everything else is considered backcountry terrain. That being the case, it's important to carry avalanche safety

WHERE TO STAY

Gulmarg is not a fancy ski area, so Khyber Himalayan Resort and Spa feels a bit out of place (it could easily have been built at Deer Valley or Beaver Creek). The rooms, equipped with large soaking tubs, have walnut paneling and are decorated with Kashmiri silk and wool carpets and hand-made furniture. The spa offers every type of massage and facial you can imagine, and large windows surrounding the indoor heated pool look out at a snowy forest.

ABOVE: Less than 6 miles (9.7 km) from the Line of Control, Gulmarg is renowned for steep mountains and heli-skiing.

OPPOSITE: Ski huts, covered in fresh snow, offer a welcome and warm break from the slopes.

equipment, and it's advisable to hire one of the ski area's experienced guides. (You should also be on the lookout for snow leopards; if you're lucky enough to spot one, give it a wide berth.)

Among the lift-serviced backcountry terrain, Hapat Khued Bowl, with its 36-degree pitches and remarkable 3,038 feet (926 m) of descent, has the best skiing and snowboarding. After getting off the second gondola, you head to the right side of the mountain, sliding past the Gondola Bowl and the Sheenmai Bowl before reaching the Hapat Khued Bowl. Winds blow light, dry snow, "reminiscent of Utah's snow," says Deane, into the bowls, consistently reloading them with deep powder. "In Hapat Khued Bowl, you can play on the sides of these natural half-pipes or ride along the tops of the spines," says Deane. "Toward the bottom, you have these perfectly spaced deciduous trees, and you can pop through them all the way back to the gondola."

DIZIN SKI RESORT

Must-Try Trail: Sichal Peak Descent

MAX ELEVATION: 11,811 feet (3,600 m)   **AVERAGE SNOWFALL: 118 inches (300 cm)**
SKIABLE TERRAIN: 1,158.9 acres (469 ha)   **OPEN SKI SEASON: December to April**

High in the central Alborz range, about 50 miles (80.5 km) north of the Iranian capital of Tehran, the country's authoritarian rule melts away, and what's left is a thriving ski and snowboard culture. "The Iranian youth go there to escape the polluted city and let loose," says Soraya Pourtabib, an Iranian American doctor who spent two seasons teaching skiing at Dizin Ski Resort. "The atmosphere is much more liberal than the rest of the country, so boys and girls feel free, flying down the slopes in short winter coats, wearing tight ski pants, their hair flowing."

Dizin became Iran's first destination ski resort when it was opened in 1968 during the rule of Mohammad Reza Pahlavi, the last shah of Iran, an avid skier who frequented its slopes. The ski area, which is located on Mount Sichal, a nearly 12,000-foot-high (3,657.6 m) peak, still feels like a bit of a throwback. Many of the lifts and gondolas, as well as some of the bunker-style stone and concrete lodges, are stuck in a late 1960s time warp. Nevertheless, over the years, Dizin has grown to include restaurants with Persian and international cuisine, cafés, rental equipment shops, hotels, chalets, hookah bars, and a ski school. (Don't expect to find any bars serving alcohol; even in the mountains, alcohol is illegal.) And—if you've crossed the hurdles required to enter Iran— there's a decent amount of skiing to be had on Dizin: More than 1,100 acres (445.2 ha) of skiable terrain offers access to 23 named runs.

KNOW BEFORE YOU GO

Traveling to Iran isn't easy. Most people are required to obtain a visa in advance (the country allows citizens from 16 nations to visit without one), and those from the United States, Canada, and the United Kingdom are allowed entrance only if they agree to be escorted by government-approved guides at all times.

OPPOSITE: **Mount Damavand looms in the distance behind the trails at Dizin.**

PAGES 270-271: **Take a break from the slopes at the base restaurant, where you can find warm drinks and local dishes.**

High above the tree line, the ski area's open, rolling bowls and long runs—up to 3,000 feet (914.4 m) long—get a fair amount of light, dry snow. "The skiing reminds me a lot of Vail," says Pourtabib. "Long and open trails that get loaded with knee-deep powder."

The difference is this: While skiers at Colorado's Vail Mountain rush to the untouched snow, tracking it out in a matter of hours, local skiers in Iran prefer to ski the resort's 15 well-groomed trails, leaving the deep snow for the limited number of outsiders—and more experienced skiers—who visit the ski area.

"There are so few people skiing outside the groomers that you can find powder turns days after a storm," says Pourtabib. "It makes you feel like you have parts of the mountain all to yourself."

The best of those powdery descents is from the top of the ski area. To get there, skiers and snowboarders ride the Chalet Gondola from the base of the mountain, then the Gholleh Gondola to the peak. When it's not snowing, the climate at

WHERE TO STAY

Dizin has two hotels that combine for 127 rooms. The modest accommodations are comfortable and look out at the ski trails, but the chalets are a more desirable lodging option. The 19 rustic, slope-side wooden houses with fireplaces and kitchens look as though they belong in the Swiss Alps and can each sleep up to five people.

ABOVE: **A skier maneuvers off-piste in Dizin's fresh powder.**

OPPOSITE: **Mount Damavand makes for an excellent view while riding the resort's gondola to numerous runs.**

the ski area is usually cold and dry, and sunny, cloudless skies allow for panoramic views of the central Alborz range, including Mount Damavand, a pyramidal peak and potentially active volcano that, at 18,605 feet (5,670.8 m), is the highest mountain in the Middle East. (The stratovolcano has a central role in Iranian mythology and folklore, and it is considered an honor for any Iranian climber to reach its summit.)

Underneath the gondola is a bowl of moderately steep terrain with some groomed trails snaking through it. And even on weeks with little falling snow, you'll find plenty of the good stuff. "Just ski to either side of the groomers, and you'll usually find a fluffy blanket of soft snow," says Pourtabib. "The bowl under the Gholleh Gondola has a vertical drop of almost 1,500 feet [457.2 m]. Then you can continue down the Chalet Bowl for another 1,500 feet [457.2 m]. A powder hound's dream."

ZAIILISKY ALATAU MOUNTAIN RANGE, KAZAKHSTAN

SHYMBULAK MOUNTAIN RESORT

Must-Try Trail: Talgar

MAX ELEVATION: 10,417 feet (3,175.1 m)   **AVERAGE SNOWFALL:** 59 inches (149.9 cm)
SKIABLE TERRAIN: 12.4 miles (20 km)   **OPEN SKI SEASON:** November to March

Shymbulak, located in the Ile Alatau mountains of southern Kazakhstan, was founded in 1954, making it one of the first alpine ski areas in the former Soviet Union. For years, it served as a training facility for Soviet ski racers, but as the Soviet Union crumbled, so did the resort. By the time Kazakhstan gained independence in 1990, the lodges had become dilapidated, and rusty chairlifts hung from the cables.

But as Kazaks began to cash in on their oil-rich economy, they began spending. In the nearby city of Almaty, skyscrapers went up, and locals began riding around in Mercedes Benzes and BMWs. They also started building huge weekend ski homes around Shymbulak. To keep up, the ski area began upgrading, constructing restaurants and hotels, bringing in the first snowmaking machines, expanding from almost 4 miles (6.4 km) of trails to more than 11 miles (17.7 km), adding lights for night skiing, and installing new lifts, including a chondola, which combines chairlifts and gondolas on the same cable. "It's more like a small European ski area now with modern lifts and dining options," says Jon Jay, an editor at SKI magazine who spent two years living in Almaty. "But it's not a huge scene. There are never lift lines."

Several trails at Shymbulak are left ungroomed, but you ski or snowboard them at your own risk. The ski area's avalanche mitigation techniques are questionable, and several inbounds slides have occurred.

OPPOSITE: A yurt houses a restaurant with authentic local cuisine at Shymbulak Mountain Resort.

PAGES 276-277: During the 2018 Gorilla Winter Jungle snowboarding and freestyle skiing festival, a boarder soars through the air.

It's probably smarter to stick to the groomed trails, 25- to 30- degree slopes that have hosted World Cup moguls competitions as well as the 2021 Freestyle Skiing World Championship. Among the best of those trails is Talgar. Named for Talgar peak—at 16,335 feet (4,978.9 m) the highest mountain in the Ile Alatau range—the trail starts at the summit of the ski area, at 10,417 feet (3,175.1 m). From the high perch, you can see much of the range, including the flanks of Chkalov Peak, a 12,769-foot-high (3,892 m) glaciated mountain, and the city of Almaty. "The views are some of the best anywhere," says Jay. "The mountains are kind of like the Alps but higher, and seeing this massive glacier spill off Chkalov Peak is an amazing sight."

As you ski down the moderately pitched slope—a 1,135-vertical-foot-descent (346 m)—you can carve through the groomed terrain or pop through some moguls on either side of the trail. "It's an easy trail that's worth skiing," says Jay, "if for no other reason than you get to experience skiing Kazakhstan, one of the wildest, most interesting places in the world."

KNOW BEFORE YOU GO

For the most part, Kazakhstan is safe, but visitors should be on the lookout for purse snatchers and pickpockets and avoid unmarked taxis. The U.S. State Department warns that passengers riding in unmarked cabs have been found unconscious after accepting laced cigarettes. The police department in Almaty also suffers from corruption, and police officers are known to stop and harass foreigners until they pay them off.

MOUNT HOTHAM

Must-Try Trail: Mary's Slide

MAX ELEVATION: 6,105.6 feet (1,861 m) **AVERAGE SNOWFALL:** 118 inches (300 cm)
SKIABLE TERRAIN: 790.7 acres (320 ha) **OPEN SKI SEASON:** June to September

With a pitch of about 35 degrees, Mary's Slide, located at Mount Hotham, a ski area in the southeastern corner of Australia, is among the steepest—if not *the* steepest—inbounds alpine trails on the continent. The big, open, treeless bowl is sheer enough, in fact, that in 1938, Mary Wallace, who'd won three Australian ski racing national championships, fell and slid all the way down the nearly 600-vertical-foot (182.9 m) run, securing the dubious honor of having the trail named for that event. "Mary's Slide can be very icy," says Coen Bennie-Faull, a professional skier who has competed on the Subaru Freeskiing World Tour and grew up skiing at Mount Hotham. "When it's like that, it's not unusual to see people falling and sliding down it. But under the right conditions, it's one of the more fun trails that I've skied anywhere in the world."

When weather patterns line up, storms blow in from the Great Australian Bight, hitting the southern portion of the Great Dividing Range and depositing up to 20 inches (50.8 cm) of snow in a 24-hour period. That's typically combined with fierce winds that flatten the snow into a smooth surface. "It creates this velvet carpet that allows for fast, floaty turns all the way down Mary's Slide," says Bennie-Faull. "Some days, when the wind is blowing really hard, you can take a run, then head back up, and the wind will have buffed out any tracks on the trail. You get to ski this blank canvas all over again."

APRÈS SKI

In Mount Hotham's village, which is uniquely situated atop the mountain (most ski resort villages are located at the bottom of the mountain), is the General, a hotel, bar, restaurant, and nightclub. To do après right, grab a drink and head out to the General's deck, where you can watch the sun set over the rolling Victorian high country.

An alpine sunrise illuminates Hotham's beloved slopes.

MOUNT NOBLE PEAK

Must-Try Trail: North Face of Sex Troll

MAX ELEVATION: 4,000 feet (1,219.2 m)   **AVERAGE SNOWFALL: Varies**
SKIABLE TERRAIN: Backcountry   **OPEN SKI SEASON: Tour dependent**

To ski the most remote mountains in the world, you first have to board a 333-foot (101.5 m) boat in Ushuaia, Argentina, and sail across the Drake Passage, a notoriously choppy, 36-hour ride that invariably turns into a floating party. "There's a great sound system, and some guy from Spain will pay for an open bar and one thing leads to another," says Andrew McLean, author of *The Chuting Gallery,* a guide to backcountry skiing in Utah, who's made 13 trips to Antarctica and helped pioneer some of the ski descents. "Next thing you know, people are dancing on the tables."

Those bacchanalian boat rides began in 1999, when Doug Stoup, a former professional soccer player turned ski and snowboard guide, started Ice Axe Expeditions and began leading trips to ski the glaciated, fang-like peaks of Antarctica. Until then, skiing in Antarctica was something experienced exclusively by polar explorers.

Since Stoup started Ice Axe, his team of 25 guides has helped hundreds of skiers and split-boarders safely trek through alleys of icebergs, past penguins and seals, and up desolate, 4,000-foot-high (1,219.2 m) peaks before descending back to the shores of the Southern Ocean, with black-browed albatross and snow petrels circling above and minke and humpback whales rising in the near distance. Ice Axe Expeditions now hosts five different Antarctic ski excursions—built around various levels of experience and lengths

CULTURAL IMMERSION

Each night, Ice Axe guests are treated to presentations from guides about skiing other far-flung places. On occasion, a guest will even get up in front of the other guests and give a talk. In 2019, George Lowe, a guest on the ship, delighted the crowd with anecdotes about his illustrious climbing career.

OPPOSITE: Skiing Antarctica means making turns around large formations of glacial ice.

PAGES 282-283: A Zodiac boat ferries visitors to a landing beach on Half Moon Island.

of trips—as well as a fat bike tour of the remote and rugged landscape.

"It's still one of the last frontiers," says Stoup. "More people have summited Mount Everest than have skied in Antarctica. These are the most surreal and visually stimulating ski runs on earth."

Among the best of Antarctica's runs is the north face of Sex Troll, a section of Mount Noble Peak on Wiencke Island, just off the west coast of the Antarctic Peninsula.

From the boat, groups of four join a guide and load onto a Zodiac for the short trip onto shore. From there, it's a 2,200-foot (670.6 m) trek up the mountain. "It takes four to five hours to climb the flank," says McLean. On the way up are views of Neumayer Channel, which splits right at the mountain and encircles the base, making it feel as though you're on a giant iceberg bobbing at sea.

Near the peak of the mountain, you'll rip off your climbing skins and prepare to descend. "It's pretty surreal to look down and see water and ice cliffs and all the rest of rugged Antarctica between the tips of your skis," says McLean.

OFF THE SLOPES

If you're not totally worked from skiing, you can hop in a kayak and take a mellow guided tour around icebergs and past emperor penguins. An onboard marine biologist will accompany you and explain Antarctica's delicate ecosystem as you paddle.

The ski down can be challenging. Antarctica gets very little snowfall, so conditions on the 50,000-year-old glacial ice that covers Sex Troll's north face can be variable—from chattery crust to sunbaked corn. The rolling slope, narrow and as steep as 45 degrees, eventually opens up into a big, open bowl, which you'll ski all the way back to the shore. "Because it's north facing, the bowl gets a lot of sun," says McLean. "So that can often be full of beautiful corn snow."

After a day of skiing and snowboarding, everybody returns to the boat—sore muscles, fantastic memories, and all—to watch the magical Antarctic sunset. "The sky is this deep dark blue and it becomes lit up red, yellow, and orange, creating this incredible contrast with the ice all around you" says McLean. "Grabbing a beer and watching that show after a day of skiing is pretty good."

ABOVE: **There are no ski resorts, chairlifts, heli-skiing, or snowcats in Antarctica—only miles of terrain accessible by human power.**

OPPOSITE: **Alpine ski mountaineers survey Antarctica's wilderness.**

PART THREE

EXPERT

A lone skier makes their way down Big Couloir, a wide-open 50-degree slope at Big Sky Resort in Montana (p. 298).

ALYESKA RESORT

Must-Try Trail: Christmas Chute

MAX ELEVATION: 4,810 feet (1,466.1 m) **AVERAGE SNOWFALL:** 669 inches (1,699.2 cm)
SKIABLE TERRAIN: 1,610 acres (651.5 ha) **OPEN SKI SEASON:** December to April

Alaska is chopper country, but there's one ski area where you can sample the state's steep couloirs without having to fly deep into the mountains. Opened on Christmas Day in 1960, Alyeska Resort, just outside the sleepy mountain town of Girdwood, is 1,610 acres (651.5 ha) of powder playground: The ski area receives an average of 669 inches (1,699.2 cm) of snow each year, the second highest amount of annual snowfall in the United States. When it's not dumping, the ski area also serves up remarkable views of the 250-mile-long (402.3 km) Chugach Range as well as Turnagain Arm, a branch of the Cook Inlet. In fact, Alyeska is one of the few ski areas in the world where you can look down between the tips of your skis at the ocean. "As one of my coaches used to say, Alyeska isn't the biggest ski area, but it has horsepower," says Tommy Moe, an Olympic gold and silver medalist who grew up skiing at Alyeska. "Steep lines and lots of snow."

The most challenging of Alyeska's terrain is located on the north face, over 400 acres (161.9 ha) of rock-lined gullies, some as steep as 50 degrees. The north face opened to the public in 1994, and although all the lines inside the bowl will take skiers and snowboarders on a wild ride, Christmas Chute—named for the time of year when the trail is typically opened—is a fan favorite.

OPPOSITE: A ski patroller and his avalanche dog monitor the slopes at Alyeksa Resort.

PAGES 290-291: Find a thriving après-ski scene at the Sitzmark Bar at the base of Alyeska.

The nearly 1,500-vertical-foot (457.2 m) run is billed as the longest continuous double black diamond run in North America. In January and February, because the sun doesn't touch the trail during those months, it's frequently filled with deep, light powder. "It can also be wind buffed, chalky, and technical," says Moe. "No matter how you get it, it will test all your skills."

To get to the trail, you ride the Glacier Bowl Express, then take a left off the chairlift, skiing a few hundred feet to a marked gate.

"The entry is the real deal," says Moe. "You're looking down at this huge convex tube that's 45 to 50 degrees steep and only 40 feet [12.2 m] wide with rock walls on either side." The chute then narrows to about 15 feet (4.6 m) wide before yawning open again. Here skiers and snowboarders have a choice: Continue down the gut of the chute or veer to the right, where there are 10- to 20-foot-high (3.1-6.1 m) cliffs to jump off.

"If you feel like getting a little air, that can be fun," says Moe. "And it often doesn't matter how you land because you're usually landing in 5 feet [1.5 m] of soft snow."

ALTERNATIVE ROUTE

You can ski the north face's deep powder without getting so rowdy. After riding the aerial tram, duck directly onto Tram Pocket, a 40-degree, wide-open face that runs directly into Chili Dog, 30 degrees of gladed trees. The two trails combine for a little more than 700 vertical feet (213.4 m) of descent.

ASPEN HIGHLANDS

Must-Try Trail: G-8

MAX ELEVATION: 12,392 feet (3,777 m)   **AVERAGE SNOWFALL:** 300 inches (762 cm)
SKIABLE TERRAIN: 1,040 acres (420.9 ha)   **OPEN SKI SEASON:** December to April

In 1958, only about 10 years after Aspen Mountain Ski Resort had begun establishing itself as America's premier destination for the wealthy, glitterati, and cultural elite, a scrappy independent ski area was founded just down the road. Aspen Highlands was the antithesis of its nearby neighbor. Food and lift tickets were cheap, and guests eschewed fur coats in favor of jean jackets. Both ski areas boast some of the best terrain in Colorado—and many would argue some of the best terrain in all of North America—but Highlands has the Highlands Bowl: some 270 acres (109.3 ha) of 35- to 48-degree steeps, open trees, and 1,000-vertical-foot (304.8 m) open faces.

For years, however, the bowl was totally off limits due to dangerous avalanche conditions. Ski patrol were even instructed to call the sheriff and have people who poached the bowl arrested. Then, in 1993, Aspen Skiing Company, owners of Aspen Mountain Ski Resort, purchased Aspen Highlands and began studying the bowl to see what it would take to safely open it to skiers and snowboarders. In 1995, using avalanche mitigation techniques including explosives and boot packing (after the first few snowfalls, hundreds of volunteers tromp around in their boots on the bowl to improve snow compaction), parts of the bowl opened. By 2002, the entire bowl was game on. Now, 18 named runs can be accessed from the ridgeline of the Highlands Bowl, all considered extremely difficult (double black) terrain.

ALTERNATIVE ROUTE

A 15- to 20-minute hike will get you to Boxcar, a 42-degree descent that's a little more than 500 vertical feet long (152.4 m). In fact, most people who hike up Highlands Bowl are heading for the peak, so by dropping in early, you have a decent chance of finding leftover powder stashes.

OPPOSITE: Skiers hike a ridgeline to reach a fresh powder trail in the resort.

PAGES 294-295: Historic Hotel Jerome, at the foot of Aspen Mountain, has been a landmark in Aspen since 1889.

But to ski it, first you have to get to it. After riding the Loge Peak chairlift to 11,675 feet (3,558.5 m), you then shoulder your skis or strap them to a pack (bowl straps—a long piece of nylon webbing that you can fashion into a carrier—can be purchased from the ski patrol shack at the top of Loge Peak) and hike approximately 700 feet (213.4 m), about 45 minutes, along a moderately steep, windy ridgeline, to the top of the 12,392-foot (3,777.1 m) peak. If you're lucky, the snowcat will be shuttling people part of the way up the ridgeline, cutting about a third off the hike. Here, you'll find prayer flags, an old chairlift seat that you can rest on and have a snack, and remarkable views of the Maroon Bells, two pinot-tinted, bell-shaped peaks that rise up more than 14,000 feet (4,267.2 m) above Maroon Lake.

There are several ways down from here, but savvy skiers in search of cold, light powder will choose the north-facing G-Zone (the name comes

APRÈS SKI

Every day at two in the afternoon, Cloud Nine Alpine Bistro, perched midmountain at 11,000 feet (3,352.8 m), hosts one of skiing's most popular parties. Near the end of the restaurant's coveted second seating, when the raclette grills and fondue pots are cleared, a DJ cranks up the hits from the '90s, patrons climb atop their chairs in ski boots, and a raucous dance party ensues, culminating with the spraying of hundreds of bottles of top-shelf Veuve Clicquot (Cloud Nine is the number one Veuve account in the country) until the place—and every ski jacket—is dripping with champagne.

from the green wax—the coldest temperature wax—needed to best slide down these slopes), a section of the bowl that gets loaded with snow thanks to westerly winds.

"You could have 4 inches [10.2 cm] of snow on the rest of the mountain but have 12 inches [30.5 cm] in the G-Zone," says Chris Davenport, a professional skier who lives in Aspen.

The longest descent in the G-Zone is G-8, accessed right from the opening of the bowl's peak gate. G-8 offers nearly 1,000 vertical feet (304.8 m) of sustained 42-degree pitch. "Highlands Bowl—like El Capitan for climbers or Mavericks for surfers—is a freak of nature for skiers," says Davenport. "And because it's steep and long, G-8 makes for one of the most exceptional ski runs in the United States. It's the closest thing to Alaska heli-skiing that we have in the lower 48."

ABOVE: **Aspen Highlands offers runs above the timberline summit of the mountain for an extra challenge.**

OPPOSITE: **Ajax (Aspen) Mountain, with its abundant trails, rises above the town of Aspen.**

BIG SKY RESORT

Must-Try Trail: Big Couloir

MAX ELEVATION: 11,166 feet (3,403.4 m)   **AVERAGE SNOWFALL:** 400+ inches (1,016+ cm)
SKIABLE TERRAIN: 5,850 acres (2,367.4 ha)   **OPEN SKI SEASON:** November to April

With 5,850 skiable acres (2,367.4 ha), Big Sky is the second largest ski area in the United States. And the Big Couloir, a 1,400-vertical-foot (426.7 m), 50-degree chute, is one of the most formidable trails in the world—so much so that in order to descend it, guests must first sign in with ski patrol and be wearing a beacon. Only groups of two can ski or snowboard the Big Couloir every 15 minutes.

"The 'Big C' cannot be compared to any other run in the lower 48," says Dan Egan, a professional skier and the star of several Warren Miller films. "Because you can only ski it in pairs, you never have to worry about a skier above you. So it's the only lift-accessed run I can think of that you can ski top to bottom and experience isolation on a steep, narrow couloir."

Big Sky was founded in 1973, and for many years skiers would hike an hour to the top of the ski area's 11,166-foot (3,403.4 m) peak in order to ski the Big Couloir. These days, the Lone Peak Tram, which opened in 1995, drops guests off atop the mountain. From there, you slide down a ridgeline to the top of the couloir, where you're faced with a decision: Jump off a large cornice or skirt around the cornice and enter the trail via a steep ramp. Once in the couloir, you officially start down the 15- to 25-foot-wide (4.6-7.6 m) trail. "You're rattling and shaking the whole way down," says Egan. "But it's an epic descent. Most of the people who ski with me consider it a run of a lifetime."

WHERE TO STAY

Lone Mountain Ranch, which is more than 100 years old, is a collection of 20 cabins, from small, quaint log constructions with wood-burning stoves to a large six-bedroom lodge that comes with a hot tub, a pool table, and two river-stone fireplaces. Outside the cabins are 50 miles (80.5 km) of groomed Nordic ski trails.

A ski racer makes her way down Big Sky's Big Couloir.

MOUNT ROSE SKI TAHOE

Must-Try Trail: El Cap

MAX ELEVATION: 9,700 feet (2,956.6 m)   **AVERAGE SNOWFALL: 350 inches (889 cm)**
SKIABLE TERRAIN: 1,200+ acres (485.6+ ha)   **OPEN SKI SEASON: November to May**

B eginning in 1964, expert skiers who visited Mount Rose—a ski area in Nevada that overlooks the clear, greenish-blue waters of Lake Tahoe—were taunted by the challenging terrain they could see while riding up the new Northwest Passage chairlift. To the left of the lift were sixteen 40- to 55-degree, powder-filled chutes, spread out across 200 acres (80.9 ha) of natural amphitheater, all roped off and closed to the public over concerns that they were extremely prone to avalanches. That, however, didn't stop skiers from poaching them. In 1972, eight skiers ducked under the ropes, setting off an avalanche that killed two people. Yet people continued to risk their lives by sneaking into the chutes.

By the late 1990s, in an effort to prevent more injuries and deaths, the ski area brass began exploring the possibility of safely opening the chutes. "We felt we could protect people more by opening them and doing proper avalanche mitigation work," says Mike Ferrari, the ski patrol manager at Mount Rose. "We also knew we needed to add terrain to make the mountain better rounded. We've always had great beginner, intermediate, and advanced skiing. Opening the chutes would give us great expert terrain too."

In 2004, the Chutes finally opened to the public, instantly becoming, among Mount Rose's 1,200 acres (485.6 ha) of skiable terrain, the star attraction. That's particularly true on powder days, which are plentiful. During the 2016-17

OPPOSITE: Mount Rose offers ideal snow conditions and 1,800 vertical feet (548.6 m) of challenges on the mountain.

PAGES 302-303: To celebrate the New Year, Mount Rose hosts a snowcat parade and fireworks show.

season, the ski area received 768 inches (19.5 m) of snow, the third highest total in the United States that year. After big dumps, skiers and snowboarders lap the Northwest Express chairlift (the Northwest Passage was replaced with a six-person lift in 2000), watching as patrollers make the chutes safe for skiing. "As we're doing mitigation work, people riding the chair have the chance to see more avalanches than at most ski areas," says Ferrari. Usually by noon the chutes are safe to enter, and skiers and snowboarders slide up to one of the nine gates that you must pass through to tackle the steep descents.

The bravest of the bunch head straight for El Cap, a nearly 1,000-vertical-foot (304.8 m) descent that's between 45 and 55 degrees steep. "It's named for the big climbing wall in Yosemite National Park," says Ferrari. "It got that name because it's the biggest, steepest thing out here." Though intimidating, the north-facing chute serves up memorable turns if you can hack it. "Even when it's not full of powder, the snow is chalky and beautiful," says Ferrari.

ALTERNATIVE ROUTE

Though still considered expert terrain, Beehive is a more wide-open, lower-angle descent than many of Mount Rose's other chutes. About 800 vertical feet (243.8 m) long and 35 degrees steep, the trail gets better sunlight than most of the other chutes and can sometimes become bumped up with moguls, making it a springtime favorite among locals, who enjoy sloshing through the slushy bumps.

TUCKERMAN RAVINE

Must-Try Trail: Left Gully

MAX ELEVATION: **6,288 feet (1,916.6 m)**   AVERAGE SNOWFALL: **315+ inches (800.1+ cm)**
SKIABLE TERRAIN: **2.9 miles (4.7 km)**   OPEN SKI SEASON: **December to April**

For over 100 years, skiers have trekked about 2.5 miles (4 km) to Tuckerman Ravine, a large, treeless amphitheater of cliffs, cornices, chutes, gullies, and 35- to 55-degree steeps carved into New Hampshire's Mount Washington. At 6,288 feet (1,916.6 m), Mount Washington is the highest peak in the northeastern United States. "It's world-class terrain," says Andrew Drummond, owner of Ski the Whites, a backcountry ski shop. "The White Mountains don't have the stature of western mountains, but when you see that steep wall, it's awe-inspiring. That's probably what drew the original skiers to it, and it's certainly what still attracts thousands of people to it each year."

Tux, as it's known, was first skied in 1913, but it became popular in the 1930s, frequented by members of the Dartmouth College ski team. In 1937, the first giant slalom ski race in the United States was held at Tux, beginning partway up the trail known as Right Gully. "They sent people up there with dynamite in April 1937 to bomb for avalanches so the racers would be safe," says Jeff Leich, the executive director of the New England Ski Museum. "It didn't work, so they held the race in the place they believed was safest, but that's probably one of the earliest examples of avalanche mitigation for skiing in the United States."

Over the years, more and more people started frequenting Mount

APRÈS SKI

About 15 minutes from the trailhead, in the town of Jackson, you'll find the Shannon Door. The Irish pub and restuarant, which was founded in 1953, serves comfort food—burgers, pizza, and nachos—along with local beers from Tuckerman Brewing Company, and features live music.

OPPOSITE: A skier makes his way down the ravine's Left Gully amid rugged terrain.

PAGES 306-307: Snowy Mount Washington serves as a backdrop for the upscale Omni Mount Washington Resort.

Washington to recreationally ski Tux, mostly in the springtime. Mount Washingtion has notoriously brutal weather (for nearly 62 years, the world record for the fastest wind gust ever recorded on the surface of the Earth—231 miles an hour/371.8 km/h—was recorded here), so scheduling a trip for a warm, sunny day in April, May, or even June is advisable.

But even on perfect days, skiing Tux is no easy task. Beginning at the Pinkham Notch Trailhead, the Tuckerman Ravine Trail is a gradual, rocky climb past the Cutler River, a trek that takes two to four hours. "For a lot of people, this is an annual pilgrimage," says Drummond. "There could easily be another 100 people on the trail with you who are also heading up to ski."

Eventually you'll reach Hermit Lake, where you'll catch your first glimpse of Tux. From here, it's about 500 feet (152.4 m) to the base of the ravine. There are typically four boot packs up the cirque, all of which access great terrain (this is avalanche territory, so before you begin hiking up,

WHERE TO STAY

If you're not opposed to roughing it, there are eight lean-tos and three tent platforms, as well as outhouses and a hand pump for water, at Hermit Lake, just below Tuckerman Ravine. Permits for the spots are available on a first-come, first-served basis at the Pinkham Notch Visitor Center at the trailhead. Nabbing one forces you to carry a lot more gear up the trail—including winter camping equipment—but it also gains you several days of easy access to skiing at Tux.

ABOVE: An ice-encrusted sign marks the summit of Mount Washington.

OPPOSITE: A boarder rides off an ice-covered cliff from the headwall at Tuckerman Ravine.

it's important that you have proper avalanche gear). But one of the most beloved runs is Left Gully.

Flanked by rocky outcroppings, the gully descends for around 900 vertical feet (274.3 m). "I love it because prevailing winds load it with snow and it's east-northeast, so it's shaded and always has a reliable snowpack," says Drummond. "The entrance is short but steep—about 50 degrees; then it mellows out to about 35 degrees."

After taking a run or two, most people post up, take a rest to eat some food, and take in the action. "You'll see every kind of skier of all abilities up there," says Drummond. "You'll see some guys land jumps off 30-foot-high [9.1 m] ice walls, and other people fall and come sliding all the way down. There's always a big crowd of spectators, and when something happens, everybody knows it."

STEVENS PASS SKI AREA

Must-Try Trail: Andromeda Face

MAX ELEVATION: 5,845 feet (1,781.6 m)   **AVERAGE SNOWFALL:** 460 inches (1,168.4 cm)
SKIABLE TERRAIN: 1,125 acres (455.3 ha)   **OPEN SKI SEASON:** December to April

People who visit Stevens Pass, located about 75 miles (120.7 km) east of Seattle and 35 miles (56.3 km) northwest of Leavenworth, come for two reasons: to ski and to snowboard. "There's not much else to do," says Ingrid Backstrom, a pro skier who lives in Leavenworth. "There's no village and no lodging at all, so the people who go there are committed, hardcore skiers who come to have fun on powder pillows, spines, and in the chutes."

Despite the lack of lodging, visitors post up at the ski area for several days, sleeping in vans or mobile homes in one of the parking lots, waiting for a storm to hit. Stevens Pass averages 460 inches (1,168.4 cm) of snowfall each season, and most of those storms come in wet, depositing heavy snow on the slopes. But the ski area is located in a convergence zone, a meteorological phenomenon in which warm ocean storms mix with cold easterly winds, resulting in snowfall that's lighter and fluffy.

The handful of times each year that happens, one of the first trails to get tagged by hungry powderhounds is Andromeda Face, a 1,066-vertical-foot (324.9 m) descent with 40-degree pitches, cliff bands, trees, and open powder fields. "It's right under the Southern Cross chairlift so it's the place to see and be seen," says Backstrom. "It's about an 18-minute ride up the lift, and you can watch people sending it, and listen to them either get heckled or cheered."

APRÈS SKI

Despite its limited infrastructure, Stevens Pass does have three day lodges. And inside the Tye Creek Lodge is the ski area's most popular après-ski bar: the Foggy Goggle. The bar's large windows look out at the ski area, allowing you to watch skiers make their last turns down the mountain. And bands and DJs are frequently cranking a variety of music.

Stevens Pass's summit, at 5,845 feet (1,781.6 m), affords visitors sweeping views of the Cascade Range.

JACKSON HOLE MOUNTAIN RESORT

Must-Try Trail: Corbet's Couloir

MAX ELEVATION: 10,450 feet (3,185 m)   **AVERAGE SNOWFALL:** 459 inches (1,165.9 cm)
SKIABLE TERRAIN: 2,500 acres (1,011.7 ha)   **OPEN SKI SEASON:** November to April

In 1963, Paul McCollister, one of the founders of Jackson Hole Mountain Resort, strapped some climbing skins to his skis and, along with Barry Corbet, a ski mountaineer and guide who'd earned a reputation making first descents throughout Wyoming's perilous Teton Range, headed to the top of Rendezvous Mountain, a 10,450-foot (3,185 m) peak within the Tetons. In a little more than two years, Jackson Hole would open to the public and McCollister was scouting potential ski trails that would become part of his new ski area. When the pair approached a couloir with a 40-degree pitch, Corbet made a declaration: "People will ski that. It will be a run." McCollister was skeptical. Just to enter the couloir, you had to either leap off or somehow slide down a 20-foot-high (6.1 m), nearly vertical cornice with jagged rocks on either side.

Nevertheless, by the 1966-67 ski season, the couloir, which McCollister had named for Corbet, was already being skied, mainly by ski patrollers and some of their friends. To get into it, they had to hold onto a rope and rappel down the sheer face of the cornice. But by the early 1980s, led by members of the Jackson Hole Air Force—a group of skiers who bombed around the mountain, taking flight whenever possible—skiers were regularly soaring off the couloir, putting on a show for the hundred or so people riding Jackson Hole's famous red tram over the couloir en route to the top of the mountain.

APRÈS SKI

Jackson Hole's most popular après-ski bar is a tourist trap. Nonetheless, no trip here is complete without a stop at the Mangy Moose. It serves up live music, smothered nachos, and an array of kitsch—from a taxidermied moose to mermaid figureheads.

OPPOSITE: Skiers stand at the edge of Corbet's Couloir, ready to make their descent.

PAGES 314-315: Saddle up to a seat at the Million Dollar Cowboy Bar in Jackson.

In 2017, the ski area began hosting the Kings and Queens of Corbet's, an event in which professional skiers and snowboarders speed off the lip of the couloir's cornice, flying 100 feet (30.5 m) through the air while performing backflips, spins, and grabs. "It feels like you're falling down an elevator shaft," says Caite Zeliff, a two-time Queen of Corbet's and a Jackson Hole resident. "It's a rough landing, but you barely think about it because the next thing you know you're skiing powder."

It's not just skiers and snowboarders who've made the leap into Corbet's. In 1999, a snowmobiler named Shad Free soared several hundred feet off the couloir. And in early June 2017, professional mountain bikers Casey Brown and Cam McCaul rode their bikes off Corbet's, landing in corn snow and careering down the 600-vertical-foot (182.9 m) trail on two wheels.

But for the general public looking for a less intimidating entrance, there's an easier way in. During the season, a luge-like rut forms on the

WHERE TO EAT

To ski Corbet's Couloir, you need to be properly fueled. On your right as you exit the tram, just a few hundred yards from the top of the couloir, is Corbet's Cabin. The tiny warming hut has seating for about 20 people and is famous for its waffles smeared with Nutella, peanut butter, lemon glaze, or brown sugar butter.

ABOVE: A skier makes first tracks in the Teton back-country just outside Jackson Hole.

OPPOSITE: A barn sits below the mountains in Grand Teton National Park.

face of the cornice. Known as the goat path, it's a fast, swooping right-hand turn that shoots you into the couloir. "Once you've made it through that, nine times out of ten, it's bliss," says Zeliff.

That's especially true if you drop into Corbet's after it has been closed for a long stretch of time. If bad weather or unstable avalanche conditions exist, ski patrol will shut down the couloir for several days as the flakes pile up. That shutdown may delay your ski by a few days, but ultimately works to your advantage. When it finally reopens, it's not uncommon to find chest-deep snow inside the gut of the couloir.

"People who visit love to ski it and get bragging rights," says Zeliff. "I get it. That couloir holds a lot of cool memories—lots of powerful moments in the history of American skiing—and when you're in it, you can feel all of that."

BANFF SUNSHINE VILLAGE

Must-Try Trail: Delirium Dive

MAX ELEVATION: 8,954 feet (2,730 m)   **AVERAGE SNOWFALL:** 364 inches (925 cm)
SKIABLE TERRAIN: 3,358 acres (1,358.9 ha)   **OPEN SKI SEASON:** November to May

The story goes like this: In the early part of the twentieth century, a skier who peered over a ridgeline near the top of Lookout Mountain—an 8,954-foot (2,730 m) peak inside Alberta's Banff National Park—looked down at the 50-degree pitches, cliffs, and chutes and declared that somebody would need to be "delirious to ski the steep cirque."

Nevertheless, by the 1970s, visitors to Sunshine Village (now known as Banff Sunshine Village) were taking a short hike from the top of the Great Divide chairlift, leaving the safe confines of the ski area boundary and making the "dive" into the technical, avalanche-prone terrain—not, however, without consequence. And so, for 20 years, Parks Canada, the organization that governs the land inside the country's national parks, closed off the area over concerns that too many skiers were getting injured while attempting the Dive. In 1998, after the ski area implemented avalanche-control techniques to make the terrain safer, the Dive was reopened. It's still a risky descent—so dicey, in fact, that in order to ski Delirium Dive, skiers are required to go with a partner and carry proper avalanche equipment, including a beacon, shovel, and probe.

But for expert skiers and snowboarders, diving in is a bucket list experience. Access to the 600-acre (242.8 ha) cirque is easy. The four-person Great

OPPOSITE: Freeskier Sven Brunso catches air on a run down Delirium Drive.

PAGES 320-321: Cascade Mountain dominates the skyline in the town of Banff.

Divide Express drops you off near the top of Lookout Mountain. (Note: As you ride up the lift, signs on a lift tower indicate that you're traveling over the Continental Divide, which separates Alberta and British Columbia.)

Once on top, you'll have expansive views of the Canadian Rockies in every direction, including Mount Assiniboine, an 11,780-foot (3,590.5 m) pyramidal peak that's right on the Continental Divide. After going through the gate into Delirium Dive and heading down a set of stairs, you can pick your poison.

Each section of the 2,000-vertical-foot (609.6 m) trail has a different name and different characteristics. Bre X, one of the first sections you'll see, has a nearly 60-degree pitch; Delirium Proper is, at 40 degrees, the "easier" way down, and is often pocked with moguls or filled with wind-scoured, chalky snow; and the Galaxy Chutes, which require a short hike to get to, are so rarely skied that they're usually full of powder. After you've picked your line—and survived the initial descent—the trail yawns out into open, mellower bowls of deep, light snow, perfect for settling your nerves.

APRÈS SKI

Mad Trapper's Smokehouse is located in the ski area's village inside a log cabin that was built in 1928. The ambience is very Canadian: servers wear flannel shirts, a taxidermied moose head hangs above a stone fireplace, and, naturally, poutine is on the menu.

LAKE LOUISE SKI RESORT

Must-Try Trail: ER 3

MAX ELEVATION: 8,650 feet (2,637 m)   **AVERAGE SNOWFALL: 179 inches (454.7 cm)**
SKIABLE TERRAIN: 4,200 acres (1,700 ha)   **OPEN SKI SEASON: November to April**

Most people know Lake Louise as home to one of the most stunning, most photographed landscapes in the world. From the steps of Fairmont Chateau Lake Louise, a 36,000-square-foot (3,344.5 sq m) luxury hotel that was built over 100 years ago inside Alberta's Banff National Park, the lake's smoky aquamarine waters (it gets its stunning color from the glaciers that feed it) stretch toward hanging glaciers covering the nearby 8,000- to 11,000-foot (2,438.4-3,352.8 m) peaks of the Canadian Rocky Mountains. Summers around Lake Louise offer hiking; the winter's frozen waters are for ice skating. But expert skiers revere the area for another reason: Lake Louise Ski Resort, which opened in 1954 and is just over 4 miles (6.4 km) northeast of the iconic hotel. The resort boasts some of the steepest, most technical inbounds ski terrain of anywhere in the world.

Many of those daring descents are found on Eagle Ridge (ER), a series of seven chutes located in the ski area's back bowls, all of them rated as double black diamond runs. "Our black diamond runs, some people would call double black diamonds," says Rocket Miller, Lake Louise's mountain manager. "Our double black diamonds are *real* double black diamonds." Most of the chutes began opening up to skiers in the late 1970s, but the trail with the most consequences, ER 3, a nearly 500-foot-long (152.4 m), 40-degree slope,

OPPOSITE: **Lake Louise Ski Resort offers loads of fresh powder and stunning vistas.**

PAGES 324-325: **The resort is known for its spectacular scenery, which can be enjoyed from its versatile terrain or the mountain's base.**

remained off-limits until the mid-1990s. "There are many other runs at Lake Louise that may be longer and as steep, but few, if any, have the character of ER 3 due to the number of difficult features," says Miller. Those features include rocky outcroppings and narrow passages through Stonehenge-like structures.

To get to ER 3, skiers and snowboarders ride the Paradise chairlift to about 8,500 feet (2,590.8 m), then traverse across "the corridor," a narrow ridge that goes to the top of ER 3. "At the top of ER 3 a sizable cornice forms," says Miller. "Some people like to launch off it into the chutes, but it's possible to ski around it." As you descend, the pitch mellows slightly, to about 35 degrees, before plunging again, sustaining a steep line until you reach a long, vertical drift of snow that forms at the bottom of lower-angle terrain that skiers and snowboarders enjoy jumping back and forth over. "Hit it during a storm, and you can get some deep powder turns in there," says Miller. "Prevailing winds are westerly, and ER 3 receives awesome leeward loading. It takes only a little snow and a bit of wind to refresh our best expert terrain."

APRÈS SKI

As the name suggests, the Lakeview Lounge inside the Fairmont Chateau Lake Louise has brilliant views of the lake. It also serves a Canadian favorite: ice wine, a wine made from grapes that are frozen on the vine. The result is a less acidic, refreshing varietal with a lower alcohol content.

COURCHEVEL SKI AREA

Must-Try Trail: Grand Couloir

MAX ELEVATION: 8,983 feet (2,738 m) **AVERAGE SNOWFALL:** 315 inches (800.1 cm)
SKIABLE TERRAIN: 1,210 acres (489.7 ha) **OPEN SKI SEASON:** December to April

With 370 miles (595.5 km) of alpine ski trails, Les Trois Vallées (The Three Valleys), a collection of eight ski areas connected by a network of lifts, is the largest ski resort in the world. The oldest of those ski areas is Courchevel, which was established in 1946 and is located in the Savoy region of the French Alps. Once full of dairy farms, and still well known for its production of Beaufort cheese, Courchevel is now a posh destination for people from all over the world, most of whom come to experience the Michelin-starred restaurants, designer boutiques, and luxury digs like Hôtel de Charme les Airelles, a slope-side hotel that looks like a cross between a palace and a gingerbread house. (Of note: There are 50 five-star hotels in France, of those, nine can be found in Courchevel.) The town of Courchevel also attracts serious skiers and snowboarders who come to challenge themselves on the mountain's steep, technical trails.

For much of that terrain, they can thank Émile Allais, a world-champion French ski racer who helped create the École Française de Ski, the ski school that every ski resort in France uses. Eight years after the ski area opened, Allais was hired as technical director, a job that put him in charge of everything from grooming to trail design. He had a goal: for the people of Courchevel to be the best skiers in the world. To do that, he felt he needed

WHERE TO STAY

Les Monts Charvin, a hotel founded in 1952 by Maurice Charvin, a Courchevel ski instructor, continues to be owned and operated by the Charvin family. The atmosphere is ski chalet cozy, with fireplaces, dark wood accents, and leather furniture in guest rooms. It's also within walking distance of the Saulire cable car.

OPPOSITE: A skier jumps from a rock while skiing off-piste in Courchevel.

PAGES 328-329: Beautiful Courchevel Street offers bars, restaurants, and shops to explore, even in fresh snow.

to create the most demanding trails for them to train on, so to that end, he established three new runs: the Gully, Émile Allais, and the Grand Couloir. All three trails were so precipitous that over the years, several people who skied them were injured. In fact, the Gully and the Émile Allais trails had to be closed to the general public in the mid-1990s due to safety concerns.

But the Grand Couloir remains open—and has over the years earned a spot on many skiing and snowboarding bucket lists, including being named one of "the world's scariest ski runs" by the *Daily Telegraph*.

The nearly 1,000-foot (304.8 m), 49-degree descent, flanked by jagged rocks on one side and a wall of snow on the other side, is a prime objective for expert skiers. "To ski most couloirs like this, you need a helicopter to get to it," says Jean-Pierre Lalanne, a ski industry veteran who calls Courchevel home.

No need for a heli-lift here. To get to the trail, you take a 20-minute ride on the Saulire cable car

OFF THE SLOPES

Aquamotion Courchevel is your one-stop shop for post-skiing recovery. In addition to indoor and outdoor pools and hot tubs, the large facility offers various types of massage, as well as cryotherapy, a process that entails standing in a shower-sized metal chamber that's pumped full of nitrogen-gas-cooled air, lowering the ambient temperature to minus 160°F (−106.7°C). It's believed that the deep freeze helps reduce inflammation and speed recovery.

from the town of Courchevel to the top of the ski area, 8,989 feet (2,738 m) above sea level. From here, you can see the Italian face of Mont Blanc—at 15,774 feet (4,808 m), the highest mountain in the Alps—as well as other glaciated peaks. The descent begins by skiing a narrow ridge with nearly 1,000-foot (304.8 m) drops on either side. "The ridge is never groomed," says Lalanne. "It's done on purpose to deter intermediates from skiing down to the couloir."

Once you make it to the top of the couloir, you can scoot to the edge, dangle the tips of your skis over it, and peer between them to eye your descent. More often than not, you'll see bumped-up, chalky snow. "Looking at it, it seems impossible to ski," says Lalanne. "People say, `No, it's too steep.' But ski it on a powder day and it's the best—skiing deep snow down a trail this steep is an experience like no other."

ABOVE: **Signs on a slope in Trois Vallées direct skiers to Courchevel or Méribel resorts.**

OPPOSITE: **Fly high above Courchevel in a hot-air balloon to get the best views.**

ROSA KHUTOR ALPINE RESORT

Must-Try Trail: Crazy Khutor

MAX ELEVATION: 7,612 feet (2,320 m) **AVERAGE SNOWFALL:** 100 inches (254 cm)
SKIABLE TERRAIN: 63.4 miles (102 km) **OPEN SKI SEASON:** December to April

When Sochi, Russia, was chosen to host the 2014 Winter Olympics, it seemed an odd choice. With a tropical climate and palm-tree-lined streets, the city, located on the shores of the Black Sea, doesn't have much of a winter vibe. In fact, it's a popular summer getaway for wealthy Russians. Despite that, in 2003 developers began constructing Rosa Khutor, a ski area with a 7,612-foot-high (2,320 m) peak that was slated to host alpine skiing events at the games.

"When we went to race there in 2012, two years before the Olympics, there was hardly even a place to stay," says Ted Ligety, a double Olympic gold medalist. "We didn't know what kind of skiing we'd find on the mountain, but as it turns out, it's probably the best ski area you'll never actually ski."

Snowfall at Rosa Khutor is feast or famine. Often, warm storms blow in off the Black Sea and spit rain on the ski area. Other times, those storms mix with cold air from the north and hang over this part of the Caucasus Mountains, dropping 5 to 6 feet (1.5–1.8 m) of snow over 72 hours. That was the case a few days before Ligety arrived at the ski area in 2012. During a day off from racing, he decided to explore the mountain.

After stepping off the Kavkazsky Express gondola at the top of the ski area, Ligety made his way down a narrow ridge before being stopped by

OPPOSITE: The Rosa Khutor Alpine Resort is a complex of hotels on the site of the former Olympic Village.

PAGES 334-335: Skiers hike to the precipice of one of many off-piste runs off the mountain.

armed military personnel. "They have bunkers up there with guns pointed at the Georgian border," he says. "During the race, security was on high alert." After explaining who he was, Ligety was allowed to pass through and eventually found himself atop Crazy Khutor, the most challenging trail on the mountain. Starting in the high alpine and eventually snaking through a dense thicket of trees that are plastered with snow, the 40- to 45-degree pitch descends for a remarkable 3,507 vertical feet (1,068.9 m). "I looked down and saw this line that looked like it could be in Alaska," says Ligety. "There was a long, steep spine and little hits and drops and it went on forever. I just wanted to keep skiing it."

When Ligety returned to Rosa Khutor a few years later for the Olympics, the village had grown to include several new shops and hotels (many were still under construction during the 2014 games). He didn't make it up to the top of the mountain again to ski Crazy Khutor, but his trip back to Rosa Khutor was still pretty good: On February 19, he won the gold medal in the giant slalom race.

KNOW BEFORE YOU GO

The reason Ted Ligety says that Rosa Khutor is "probably the best ski area you'll never actually ski" is that it's hard to get to. Flights from the United States can take more than 24 hours and require several stops. In addition, the U.S. State Department warns American travelers to Russia to be wary of "terrorism, harassment, and the arbitrary enforcement of local laws."

TREBLE CONE SKI AREA

Must-Try Trail: Chute 9

MAX ELEVATION: 6,850 feet (2,088 m)   **AVERAGE SNOWFALL:** 216 inches (548.6 cm)
SKIABLE TERRAIN: 1,359 acres (550 ha)   **OPEN SKI SEASON:** June to September

Treble Cone is like a 1,359-acre (550 ha) terrain park. Started in 1968 by a small group of skiing enthusiasts, it's now the largest ski area on New Zealand's South Island and is known for supersized, au natural X Games–like features—1,000-foot-long (304.8 m) half-pipes, gullies, lips, and drops—that encourage skiers and snowboarders to jump, flip, and spin their way through the mountain.

The most popular descents on the mountain are the Motatapu Chutes, a series of 40- to 45-degree descents separated by large rock walls. "It's kind of like this huge claw system of big fingery ridges," says Sam Smoothy, a pro skier who grew up skiing at Treble Cone. "There are all these hidden gems in there—little ramps and sidewalls that you can billy-goat around on."

Among the chutes, Chute 9 stands out. About 500 vertical feet long (152.4 m), the trail is wider than some of the other chutes, allowing for bigger turns. To get to the chute, you take the Saddle Basin Quad to 6,430 feet (1,959.9 m), then ski down the south ridge toward Gate 2. After making it through the vertical playground, you exit into Motatapu Basin, where you'll need to shoulder your skis and hike for 15 to 20 minutes back to the lift. Or you can retreat to the ski area's small base lodge, where you can take in views of the country's southern alps, lush rainforests, and Lake Wanaka, New Zealand's fourth largest lake, while enjoying a beverage among the keas, native mountain parrots.

OFF THE SLOPES

Lake Wanaka's Glendhu Bay is just a short drive from Treble Cone. The crescent-shaped inlet has stony beaches, poplar trees, and easy access to the lake's impossibly clear water. "After skiing in the spring [September through November in New Zealand], we'll jump in the lake," says Smoothy. "It's still cold, but it feels so good after a long day at the mountain."

From the crest of a slope at Treble Cone, skiers can catch views of Lake Wanaka.

XIAOHAITUO MOUNTAIN

Must-Try Trail: Olympic Downhill Course

MAX ELEVATION: **7,214 feet (2,198.8 m)**   AVERAGE SNOWFALL: **8.3 inches (21 cm)**
SKIABLE TERRAIN: **6.2 miles (10 km)**   OPEN SKI SEASON: **Unknown**

Despite the fact that Xiaohaituo Mountain—a 7,214-foot-high (2,198.8 m) peak that's just 55 miles (88.5 km) from Beijing—receives very little natural snowfall and had no ski trails until very recently, in February 2022, the brand-new ski area will host the downhill event at the Winter Olympics on a course that Bernhard Russi, an Olympic downhill gold medalist and architect of several Olympic and World Cup tracks, is calling one of the best downhill race courses in the world.

Construction of the ski area began in 2017 and was done in an environmentally friendly way. During the building of roads, lifts, trails, a network of snowmaking pipes, and various other infrastructure, workers installed temporary migration paths for local animals. Rather than swinging axes, thousands of trees—consisting of 30 different species—were uprooted and transplanted at the bottom of the mountain or at other places.

To ski or snowboard down the trail, you ride a gondola to the top of the mountain, docking in a station that looks like a kite ready to fly down the course. You might feel as though you're flying down it too. Pitches as steep as 68 degrees and slick man-made snow make for fast conditions. "It's a technical trail with lots of doglegs and bends and steep drop-offs," says Steven Nyman, a member of the U.S. Ski Team. "It's going to make for a great race and a fun trail to ski when the gates are gone, too."

CULTURAL IMMERSION

Just a little over 10 miles (16.1 km) from downtown Yinqing is Badaling, the most visited section of the Great Wall of China. Built during the Ming dynasty in the early 1500s, it was the first section of the wall opened to tourists in 1957. These days, it's often mobbed with people; however, wintertime crowds are lighter, making it a perfect cultural experience after a day of skiing.

Despite receiving very little natural snow, Xiaohaituo Mountain is one of the sites of the 2022 Winter Olympic Games.

PART FOUR

CROSS-COUNTRY

Find otherworldly landscapes on a
skate across Spencer Glacier near
Portage, Alaska (p. 342).

SKOOKUM GLACIER

Must-Try Trail: Skookum Glacier Crust Skiing

MAX ELEVATION: 1,014 feet (309.1 m)   **AVERAGE SNOWFALL: 241 inches (612.1 cm)**
SKIABLE TERRAIN: 4 miles (6.4 km)   **OPEN SKI SEASON: Mid-April to mid-May**

They call it crust skiing, and you'll hear Alaskan cross-country skiers rave about the short, magical window of time each year during which it's possible. They'll tell you that the unique experience is euphoric—that it makes you feel as if you're flying.

"I call it hero snow, because it makes you feel like an awesome skier," says Kikkan Randall, who grew up in Anchorage and won a gold medal in cross-country skiing at the 2018 Winter Olympics. "You don't have to be elite; it makes everybody feel that good. And you can go really fast."

The genre gets its name from the icy crust that forms overnight on the surface of the snow. For decades, between about mid-April and mid-May—the only time of year that the crust forms—Alaskans have taken advantage, using skate skis to soar across the smooth, supportive surface in the same way that ice-skaters glide across a lake.

One of the more popular places to crust-ski is on the Skookum Glacier on the Kenai Peninsula, just a 40-mile (64.4 km) drive southeast from Anchorage on the Seward Highway. To find the way in, you'll need a GPS device or, better yet, a guide who can also steer you clear of hidden crevasses that scar the glacier. And to nail the snow conditions, you'll need to leave early in the morning; by about noon, the sun has melted the crust into a sloppy, difficult-to-ski slush.

OPPOSITE: Cross-country skiers make their way across frozen Portage Lake with Bard Peak in the background.

PAGES 344-345: A faint aurora borealis hovers above a campsite on Skookum Glacier.

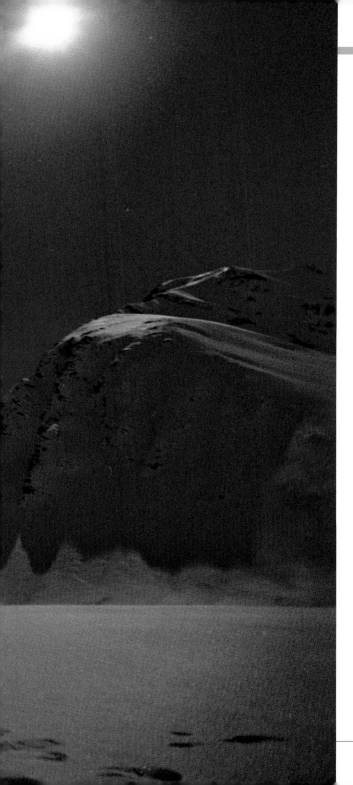

From the road, you'll follow the Placer River Valley to the Skookum Creek, which will lead to the glacier. Along the 3-mile-long (4.8 km) ski, you'll pass a tree graveyard, the remnants of a 1964 earthquake that caused the ground level to drop 9 feet (2.7 m), flooding this valley with ocean water that killed the still-standing gray and gnarled forest.

From there, it's past a 100-foot-high (30.5 m) ice cliff and onto the glacier, where you're surrounded by the peaks of the Kenai Mountains. There are no trails here.

"It's choose your own adventure," says Randall. "The glacier is like a giant playground of natural half-pipes and little dips and turns."

On the crusted surface, you'll travel twice the speed you normally would, which means that making it to the end of the 4-mile-long (6.4 km) glacier can take as little as 10 minutes. There, you'll find ice caves, stunning blue-ice walls, and giant columns of blue ice.

Says Randall: "It's so much fun and so beautiful that you'll be out there for three hours and it doesn't feel like any time has passed at all."

WHERE TO EAT

The rules at Chair 5 in Girdwood, Alaska, not far from Skookum Glacier, are clear: "Absolutely No Gunfights, Fist Fights, Food Fights, or Cursing," reads a sign in the restaurant. After a long ski, this is your best opportunity to refuel with triple-decker burgers, pizza, and other comfort food.

DEVIL'S THUMB RANCH

Must-Try Trail: Lactic Grande to Waxwing

MAX ELEVATION: 8,405 feet (2,561.8 m) **AVERAGE SNOWFALL: 163 inches (414 cm)**
SKIABLE TERRAIN: 74.6 miles (120 km) **OPEN SKI SEASON: November to March**

Despite being just an hour-and-a-half from Denver and right down the road from Winter Park Resort, Devil's Thumb Ranch feels remote. The property sits in a quiet valley, spread out across 6,500 acres (2,630.5 ha) of windswept fields and dense forest. The ranch was built in the 1930s and was named for the Devil's Thumb, a prominent rocky outcropping that juts out from the Indian Peaks Wilderness. (Legend has it that after decades of fighting, the Utes and Arapahoe declared peace and buried the devil, leaving only his thumb exposed.) In 1975, former Olympic ski racer Dick Taylor began developing cross-country ski trails on the land.

Over the years, that's expanded to almost 75 miles (120.7 km) of groomed trail, the best of which are Lactic Grande and Waxwing. Accessing the trails requires an easy 3-mile (4.8 km) ski along three warm-up runs—Blue Extra, Double Pole, and Disco—to the Lactic Grande trailhead, located on the southeastern edge of the property. From there, it's a 2-mile (3.2 km), 25-degree climb to the ranch's highest point, the best spot to take in views of Byers Peak, the highest nearby mountain, and the sinuous Fraser River. Then it's a harrowing 30-degree, mile-long (1.6 km) descent that leads to Waxwing, a trail that meanders for 2 miles (3.2 km) through lodgepole pines and aspens. Here, besides the breeze through the trees, the babbling of a nearby brook, or the rustling of a moose, you'll discover utter silence and blissful isolation.

WHERE TO STAY

When new owners purchased Devil's Thumb in 2001, the entire ranch underwent a major renovation. That included a full-service spa, a game room with a two-lane bowling alley, private cabins, and several restaurants, including Heck's Tavern, which serves gourmet twists on comfort food, like Wagyu meatloaf. Best of all, you're just steps from the ski trails.

Cross-country skier Jon Kruper makes his way up a trail to the main lodge at Devil's Thumb Ranch.

WOLVERINE NORDIC TRAILS

Must-Try Trail: The Cliff and Cliffhanger

MAX ELEVATION: 1,506 feet (459 m)   **AVERAGE SNOWFALL:** 200 inches (508 cm)
SKIABLE TERRAIN: 15 miles (24.1 km)   **OPEN SKI SEASON:** December to April

When the glaciers that carved out most of Michigan's Upper Peninsula receded two million years ago, they left behind rolling hills and the largest freshwater lake in the world, Superior, which produces lake-effect snowstorms that blanket the region with some 200 inches (508 cm) of snow each year. The snow and topography, along with long, cold winters, make for ideal cross-country skiing conditions. So when a number of Finns and Swedes emigrated to the Upper Peninsula, bringing their Nordic traditions with them, it was no surprise that they cut hundreds of miles of trails to slide along .

Some of the best trails are found in the Wolverine Nordic Trail System, a 15-mile (24.1 km) network of tracks on the Wisconsin border that are known for their consistently good grooming (for both skate and classic skiing) and the fact that during the ski season, they're open 24 hours a day, seven days a week.The gems of the system are the Cliff and Cliffhanger trails.

Though a daytime ski through the poplar, aspen, spruce, and white birch trees is nice, skiing them at night is an otherworldly experience. That's particularly true when you get to the cliff section of the Cliff Trail, where the rocky outcroppings bordering the trail are plastered with ice and the minerals that have created a kaleidoscope of frozen colors: light browns, yellows, and reds that, when reflecting light, looks like something out of a Disney theme park.

WHERE TO EAT

Founded in the 1970s, Don & GG's serves classic Upper Peninsula food to hardened locals in Carhartt uniforms as well as hungry Nordic skiers who've been frequenting the restaurant since it opened, refueling on cheese curds, fish fry, and burgers like the Lumberjack: house-shaved prime rib and cheddar jack on a grilled pretzel bun.

A skier and dog both enjoy the fresh snow on groomed cross-country trails.

KORKKI NORDIC SKI CENTER

Must-Try Trail: The 10KM Loop

MAX ELEVATION: 702 feet (214 m) **AVERAGE SNOWFALL:** 70 inches (177.8 cm)
SKIABLE TERRAIN: 6.8 miles (11 km) **OPEN SKI SEASON:** January to April

Around the middle of the 19th century, when large numbers of Scandinavians began immigrating to the United States in search of better jobs and a chance to own their own property, many ended up in Minnesota. To make themselves feel more at home, several of the newcomers, who'd practically been raised on cross-country skis, began building ski trails in their backyards.

In keeping with that tradition, Charlie Banks, a popular cross-country ski racer with Finnish roots, used an ax and grub hoe to craft a tangle of single-track behind his house in Duluth in 1954. For the most part, Banks allowed only friends, family, and a handful of local ski racers (who'd use the small network as a training ground) to ski his trails. He also hosted ski races, including the Erik Judeen Memorial Classic (named for Banks's former coach), a 6.2-mile (10 km) event that was started in 1963 and grew to become one of the biggest ski races in the Midwest, even drawing international talent from Italy, Germany, Russia, and Canada.

In 1992, Mark Helmer, a local skier who'd met Banks and started using his trails a decade earlier, suggested that he open the beloved network of trails to the public.

"His wife had died, and he was retired, and I thought that it would give him something to do," says Helmer. Helmer offered to help and suggested

WHERE TO EAT

The New Scenic Café has been a favorite Lake Superior restaurant since it opened in 1999. Inside a timber-frame dining room, under chandeliers that look like big snowballs, chef Scott Graden serves several Scandinavian favorites, such as Swedish meatballs and beet-cured gravlax.

OPPOSITE: Thanks to Lake Superior, Duluth receives plenty of winter snow.

PAGES 352-353: The Korkki Nordic Ski Center has been a beloved part of Duluth for generations.

they call the ski area Korkki Nordic, named for the Finnish family who'd homesteaded the property in the early 1900s.

These days, other than a small warming hut that was constructed in 1993, the 6.8-mile (11 km) trail network is much the same as when Banks built it. Only wide enough for classic skis (Helmer can't ever see widening the trails enough to accommodate skating), the nonprofit draws skiers who come to test their skills on the original 10-km loop where the Erik Judeen Memorial Classic was first held.

"It's like skiing in a snow globe—a winter wonderland," says Chad Salmela, a former member of the U.S. Biathlon Team who now calls Olympic biathlon and cross-country races for NBC. "There's almost always a layer of frost on the deciduous and boreal forest, and when the sun is shining, the trees glitter."

The trail is composed of brutal climbs, steep, flume-like descents, and sharp turns, and each section has its own name and a little story to go along with how it was christened. For example, Cook's Fall is named after Sam Cook, a Duluth local

WHERE TO STAY

About 10 miles (16.1 km) from Korkki Nordic, right on the frozen shoreline of Lake Superior, are the Larsmont Cottages. Located on 40 acres (16.2 ha) of wooded landscape, the property is a warm antidote to a cold day on the trails: Each cottage has fireplaces and whirlpool tubs, as well as access to a heated indoor swimming pool and a wood-fired sauna.

who came zipping down this part of the hill as Charlie and Mark Helmer were grooming the roller coaster–like section. Cook barely missed the groomer, and instead barreled face-first into the deep snow on the trail, earning himself a name on the way down.

There's also Salmela's Curve, which was the scene of a legendary incident in which Chad Salmela went too fast into the curve, taking out a number of other skiers and causing a pileup.

"The best part of the trail is the descent from Iso Maki [Finnish, meaning 'big hill']," says Salmela. "The views of Lake Superior from the top are magical. And the ski down is a screamer—you can go 25 to 30 miles an hour [40.2 to 48.3 km/h]. If you're there on a Saturday when a lot of people are out skiing, you'll hear them screaming 'whooo' all day, and you know exactly where they are on the course."

ABOVE: The inside of the Korkki Nordic Ski Center is decorated with old photos, ski bibs, skis, and memorabilia.

OPPOSITE: During a winter storm, Lake Superior waves roll onto the shoreline at Split Rock Lighthouse.

RIKERT NORDIC CENTER

Must-Try Trail: Tormondsen Trail

MAX ELEVATION: 1,680 feet (512.1 m) **AVERAGE SNOWFALL: 122 inches (309.9 cm)**
SKIABLE TERRAIN: 34.2+ miles (55+ km) **OPEN SKI SEASON: December to April**

The woods tucked beneath Bread Loaf Mountain drip with Vermont charm: as you cross-country ski along the trails here, you'll slide through maple groves and farm fields, over babbling brooks, and past stone walls, as well as the former summer cabin of famed poet Robert Frost. Frost was drawn to this part of New England in 1921 and spent summers teaching at Middlebury College's School of English (founded in 1920) until his death in 1963. The land where the English program was located had been a dairy farm, owned by Joseph Battell, who donated all 31,000 acres (12,545.3 ha) to the college in 1915. Over the years, most of the land was sold off, and today, 1,800 acres (728.3 ha) are home to Middlebury's Bread Loaf campus and the Rikert Nordic Center's 34 miles (55 km) of trails.

The best skiing is on the Tormondsen Trail, which was designed by John Morton, a noted cross-country trail builder who has created Nordic networks all over the country. It opened in 2011 and added snowmaking in 2012—10 to 15 snow guns that each blow 250 gallons (946.4 L) a minute. That same year, the NCAA skiing championships were held on the trail, and it has been used for countless races since.

But there's no need to race through the 3.1-mile (5 km) loop. It's better, in fact, to take it slow and enjoy its features. "It's wide—about 30 feet wide

OPPOSITE: The Rikert Nordic Center's yellow buildings are set in the picturesque Vermont countryside.

PAGES 358-359: College athletes battle for first place during the men's Nordic freestyle competition at the 2013 NCAA Division I championship.

[9 m]—and it's skier-friendly, even for nonracers," says Andrew Johnson, a former member of the U.S. Ski Team and current Middlebury College coach. "Most race trails aren't that way, but this one is."

The trail starts by crossing a creek over a wood bridge, then eventually snakes down a moderately steep chicane. From there you climb through maples on the Sugarhouse Loop, where a sugar shack used for making maple syrup once stood, before descending a steeper, more technical hill. "It's a real lung-buster climb," says Johnson. "Then you have to make sure you're not too tired to make it through some quick turns on the downhill."

The final section is a 1.2-mile (1.9 km) loop over easy, rolling terrain. "It's my favorite part because it's just a nice gradual grade that anybody can go ski," says Johnson. "If you're a beginner, you could just go ski this last loop and have a good time." Ideally, you're finishing the trail as the sun is setting so that you can watch Bread Loaf Mountain, a long, rounded peak that resembles a loaf of bread, light up pink in the evening alpenglow.

WHERE TO STAY

The Swift House, in the town of Middlebury (only about 20 minutes from the Nordic Center), was built in 1814 and the main federal-style building maintains much of its 19th century charm—rooms with floral wallpaper, cherry wood furnishings, and fireplaces—without skimping on modern conveniences, such as jetted bathtubs and a community sauna.

METHOW TRAILS

Must-Try Trail: Rendezvous Trail System

MAX ELEVATION: 2,118 feet (645.6 m)   **AVERAGE SNOWFALL:** 88 inches (223.5 cm)
SKIABLE TERRAIN: 125 miles (201.2 km)   **OPEN SKI SEASON:** December to April

Had the Aspen Skiing Company succeeded in building what it called "the best potential destination ski resort in the United States," Washington's Methow Valley, which runs 70 miles (112.7 km) from the arid Columbia River basin to the verdant North Cascades, wouldn't be the secluded, tranquil valley it is today. In the mid-1970s, Methow locals enlisted help from Seattle environmental groups, including the Sierra Club, and after decades of lawsuits—one of which made it to the U.S. Supreme Court—fought off chairlifts, condos, and a base village. Opting instead for human-powered skiing as its economic driver, the Methow Valley developed North America's largest cross-country ski area, connecting its small towns with more than 125 miles (201.2 km) of groomed Nordic trails, preserving its rural setting, and creating an invested community—as well as multiple Olympians.

"One of my favorite aspects of the Methow is that when you go for a ski, you go for an adventure," says Sadie Maubet Bjornsen, who skied for the Methow Valley Nordic Ski Educational Foundation and competed in the 2014 and 2018 Winter Olympics. "You don't just ski a loop and arrive at the same place. Often you're skiing from one town to the next. Or you're skiing up and over a mountain pass. Or you're skiing from one coffee shop or bakery to another. You have unlimited options."

APRÈS SKI

After skiing, you've earned yourself a Manhattan, or a Paper Airplane, or a Negroni, or one of the many other cocktails that are carefully crafted at Copper Glance, a cozy establishment in Winthrop, Washington, that also serves tasty snacks, like house pickles and Gruyère mac and cheese.

OPPOSITE: Find warming huts for quick breaks as you make your way along the Methow Valley trails.

PAGES 362-363: There are miles and miles to explore in Methow Valley's cross-country landscape.

The vast majority of trails are beginner or intermediate terrain, including the region's most popular attraction: the Community Trail, an 18-mile-long (29 km), mostly gentle stretch that runs north from the southern end of Methow Valley, meandering along the crystal clear Methow River, ending in the town of Mazama (reward yourself by buying a famous sea salt baguette, smeared with homemade goat cheese, from the beloved ski-in, ski-out Mazama Store).

The U-shaped valley's most challenging, most scenic adventure is had by skiing the 37 miles (59.5 km) of groomed track that make up the Rendezvous Trail System, rolling terrain full of sharp turns and fast downhills that snakes through ponderosa pine forests and climbs 2,000 feet (609.6 m) from the valley floor to the flanks of Rendezvous Mountain. Almost always clear (the Methow Valley averages 300 days of sunshine each year), the high perch from this loop offers some of the region's best views of the North Cascades' jagged peaks (nicknamed "America's Alps").

Though it's possible to bang out the whole loop in a single day, the best way to experience

WHERE TO EAT

People can live on ramen noodles for only so long. After spending several days on the Rendezvous Trails, the perfect antidote to easy-to-make hut food and energy bars is a gourmet meal from Arrowleaf Bistro in Winthrop, Washington. On the menu are specialties like wild boar Bolognese and roasted chili-rubbed venison.

ABOVE: Enjoy a candlelit
meal at the Rendezvous
Huts after a day of skiing.

OPPOSITE: Along one route,
skate across one of the valley's suspension bridges.

the system of trails is by staying overnight in the Rendezvous Huts, a network of five wood-frame shelters spaced 5 miles (8 km) apart. Built between the 1980s and 1990s, each spartan hut has a wood-burning stove, a full kitchen with a propane stove and oven as well as pots and pans, and bunk beds that sleep eight to 10 people. There's also a sanitary outhouse adjacent to each hut. And although you can haul in food and bedding on a sled attached to your waist, for a fee, freight haulers will transport your gear—up to 300 pounds (136.1 kg) of it—via snowmobile to each hut.

"The huts are a special part of the Methow because the reward for your effort is that you get to sleep in these cozy little cabins, miles and miles away from the next closest guest," says Maubet Bjornsen. "At this point, I've skied all over the world, and the hut experience is just another reason I still consider Methow one of the best Nordic ski destinations out there."

GRAND TETON NATIONAL PARK

Must-Try Trail: Jackson Lake–Colter Bay Island Hopping

MAX ELEVATION: 6,887 feet (2,099.2 m)   **AVERAGE SNOWFALL: 175 inches (444.5 cm)**
SKIABLE TERRAIN: 6 miles (9.7 km)   **OPEN SKI SEASON: January to April**

The Tetons, a 40-mile-long (64.4 km) mountain range in western Wyoming, are coveted by alpine skiers and mountaineers who gather there to test their skills on the jagged peaks. The highest and most famous is Grand Teton, a 13,776-foot (4,198.9 m) spire that typically takes several days—and requires significant rock-climbing skills—to scale.

But there's no need to risk life or limb to enjoy the mountains. In fact, one the best ways to view the Tetons is by cross-country skiing onto frozen, snow-covered Jackson Lake, a 40-square-mile (103.6 sq km) body of water where a monochrome sea of white gives way to unobstructed views of several peaks, including Grand Teton, Mount Owen, and Mount Teewinot.

The ski, which begins in Grand Teton National Park's Colter Bay, can be done between January and early April, when the lake is thoroughly frozen. And though there's no trail to follow, JH Nordic, a local nonprofit, provides a detailed map of the route on its website, and the 6-mile (9.7 km) loop around part of the eastern shoreline is easy to navigate using GPS. As you weave around small, densely forested islands, you might spot moose or deer. Something you're unlikely to see? Other people. The remoteness of the tour, along with the fact that you'll likely be breaking trail through deep snow (thus putting forth a bit more effort than the general population cares to exert), practically ensures solitude.

APRÈS SKI

By now you think you've had your fill of Teton views, but it's still worth stopping at Dornan's Chuckwagon, a 73-year-old restaurant on the shores of the Snake River, inside Grand Teton National Park. The food is so-so, but since Grand Teton seems so close that it feels like you could reach out and touch it, there's perhaps no place better to sip an après beer.

A woman skis across a set trail in the vast landscape of Colter Bay.

SOVEREIGN LAKE NORDIC CLUB

Must-Try Trail: Lars Taylor Way to Silver Queen to Prince of Wales to Aberdeen

MAX ELEVATION: 5,394 feet (1,664 m) **AVERAGE SNOWFALL:** 276 inches (700 cm)
SKIABLE TERRAIN: 65+ miles (104.6 km) **OPEN SKI SEASON:** October to May

With some 65 miles (104.6 km) of trails, Sovereign Lake Nordic Club and Silver Star Mountain Resort, two adjacent ski areas in south-central British Columbia that operate in unison, have the largest continuously groomed network of cross-country ski trails in Canada. "It's not just that they're all groomed; it's that the grooming is world class," says Glenn Bond, an elite cross-country ski coach. "They use state-of-the-art machines to buff out wide tracks, and they really know what they're doing. It's one of the top cross-country ski areas in North America."

Several elite ski racers would agree. The trails at Sovereign Lake Nordic Club and Silver Star Mountain Resort have each hosted World Cup ski races, and prior to the 2010 Winter Olympics, which took place almost 280 miles (450.6 km) away at Whistler, British Columbia, more than a dozen national teams chose to use the trails as their training grounds.

The most challenging loop skirts the exterior of the Sovereign Lake trail system, a nearly 10-mile (16.1 km) tour along Lars Taylor Way, Silver Queen, Prince of Wales, and Aberdeen. "It's like a roller coaster," says Bond. "It's fast and fun with big climbs, big descents, and lots of twists and turns." Along the way, you'll look out at views of the jagged Monashee Mountains and pass huge spruce trees and cedar trees with spiderweb-like moss hanging from them and lodgepole pines that are coated with rime ice.

WHERE TO EAT

To fuel up before your ski or after it, the Bugaboos Bakery Cafe is there for you. As you walk around the Silver Star Mountain village, you're likely to hear people chattering about the local institution's cinnamon rolls, sausage rolls, and fresh Italian coffee.

Mont-Sainte-Anne Cross-Country Ski Centre features more than 114 miles (183.5 km) of trails, one of the largest systems in North America.

OLYMPIAREGION SEEFELD

Must-Try Trail: The Olympic Track

MAX ELEVATION: 3,937 feet (1,200 m)   **AVERAGE SNOWFALL: 172 inches (436.9 cm)**
SKIABLE TERRAIN: 152 miles (244.6 km)   **OPEN SKI SEASON: December to April**

There's perhaps no other country thicker with alpine ski culture than Austria. As the birthplace of Anton Seelos, the inventor of the parallel turn, the tiny town of Seefeld, tucked into the eastern Alps, plays no small role in that legacy. But in 1964, when nearby Innsbruck hosted the Winter Olympics, the rolling hills and high plateaus of Seefeld made the town the ideal venue for cross-country skiing events. Since then, Seefeld has developed 152 miles (244.6 km) of groomed trails, is renowned for its reliable snowpack, and has hosted cross-country skiing at another Olympic Games (1976) as well as two Nordic World Championships (1985 and 2019). In short, Seefeld hasn't only become the cross-country skiing outpost of an alpine-crazy nation; it's one of the premier cross-country ski destinations in the world.

It may be unsurprising that the best skiing in Seefeld is on the former Olympic and World Championship track, comprising 11 different trails groomed for both skate and classic skiing. Don't let the uninspired trail names—C1, B2, and A3, for example—deter you. The approximately 14-mile (22.5 km) loop is anything but dull as it passes through evergreen forests (keep an eye out for roe deer and foxes), over high-altitude meadows lined with weathered farm fencing, and past frozen lakes and Tyrolean restaurants, much of the time with views of rocky, snowy peaks.

OPPOSITE: Austria's looming mountains offer a scenic backdrop for a large network of cross-country trails.

PAGES 372-373: Seefeld's cross-country skiing area offers classic and skating-style tracks that are freshly groomed daily.

The ski tour starts near the center of town, inside the stadium used for the World Championship races in 2019. (Should the mood strike after the sun goes down, the 2.5-mile/4 km, undulating track inside the stadium is equipped with lights for night skiing.)

From there, it climbs to the Wildmoosalm, a restaurant that is most easily accessible by skis during the winter (in the summer, hiking and biking trails lead to the beloved establishment and its well-used sun terrace). The restaurant is decorated with antler chandeliers, taxidermied boar and deer heads, cow bells, and flags, and there's a schnapps fountain that's constantly flowing with the favored spirit of Austria. During your ski, it's likely best to skip the fountain and grab some strudel.

After your quick bite and the chance to rest your legs, head through the forest and past Wildmoossee Lake, then Lottensee Lake. Along the way, you'll glide past mushers driving sled dogs and views of the Karwendel Range, the largest mountain range of the Northern Limestone Alps, before looping back into town.

OFF THE SLOPES

After a long ski, Olympiabad Seefeld, located near the center of town, is the type of place your muscles crave. A large heated pool, complete with massaging jets, several different types of saunas, and a cold plunge, should restore your strength. And if you're looking for a little more excitement, you can try one of the water slides, which are open year-round.

SEISER ALM

Must-Try Trail: Link Trail Saltria–Monte Pana

MAX ELEVATION: 7,710 feet (2,350 m)   **AVERAGE SNOWFALL: 98 inches (250 cm)**
SKIABLE TERRAIN: 50 miles (80.5 km)   **OPEN SKI SEASON: December to April**

Seiser Alm (also known as Alpe di Siusi), a 20-square-mile (51.9 sq km) plateau located 5,600 feet (1,706.9 m) above sea level in northern Italy, is the highest alpine meadow in Europe. The rolling hills—with patches of evergreens and home to roe and red deer, foxes, hares, and chamois—have streams and rivers meandering through them and are surrounded by the spires and shark-fin peaks of the Dolomites. "If you close your eyes and picture the perfect layout for cross-country skiing, that's what Seiser Alm is," says Kevin Bolger, a member of the U.S. Nordic Ski Team. "You have all these twisty, turny Nordic trails snaking through the whole region, and there's hardly anybody here using them. It's like a hidden gem."

There are almost 50 miles (80.5 km) of groomed cross-country trails in Seiser Alm, but the most challenging terrain is found on the 2.5-mile (4 km) stretch of the Link Trail Saltria–Monte Pana. The trail begins in an open meadow and descends toward the woods. After crossing a bridge, you ski along a river, across an icy part of the route, then climb for about a mile (1.6 km) before reaching an exposed section of trail. "You're going downhill on a narrow ribbon of terrain for about half a mile [0.8 km] with steep, rocky pitches on one side and incredible views of massive mountains in front of you," says Bolger. "It's a short loop, but it has a little bit of everything: fast downhills, tough climbs, and amazing scenery."

WHERE TO STAY

The Link Trail Saltria–Monte Pana starts right outside Hotel Saltria, a stone and wood construction with a classic Tyrolean motif. The hotel has a swimming pool, hot tubs, and saunas, as well as daybeds lined up behind huge windows that look out on the Dolomites. And the restaurant serves local dishes, such as spaghetti Bolognese, wiener schnitzel, and bratwurst.

Stars illuminate the cross-country trail on the Alpe di Siusi mountain plateau.

RONDANE NATIONAL PARK

Must-Try Trail: Troll Trail

MAX ELEVATION: 3,280 feet (1,000 m) **AVERAGE SNOWFALL: Unknown**
SKIABLE TERRAIN: 96 miles (155 km) **OPEN SKI SEASON: November to May**

Cross-country skiing most likely began in Russia about 8,000 years ago, but no other country's culture is more entwined with the sport than Norway, where sliding around on skinny skis is the national pastime. "Everybody skis," says Andy Newell, a former U.S. Ski Team member. "And people go everywhere with their skis. Even if you're a banker sitting at your desk all week, you go out and ski 25 kilometers [15.5 mi] on the weekend." The country has more than 18,000 miles (28,968 km) of marked cross-country ski trails. The most famous of those is the Birkebeiner, a 33.5-mile-long (54 km) trail that runs between the towns of Rena and Lillehammer.

The Troll Trail, a 96-mile (155 km) trek from Rondane National Park in central Norway, also finishing in Lillehammer—site of the 1994 Winter Olympics—is among those considered Norway's best multiday tours. Alone or with an outfitter, you begin on frozen tundra, among wild reindeer. The groomed trail wends over hills and through birch forests, and along the route are woodstove-heated timber cabins, some with thatch roofs; quaint hotels that serve up scrambled eggs, smoked salmon, and brown cheese (a Norwegian staple) breakfasts; and even major resorts. After six or seven days of skiing (the average time it takes most people to complete the Troll Trail), you'll arrive on the shores of Lake Mjøsa in Lillehammer, a resort town with buildings dating back to the 1200s and a ski shop around every corner.

APRÈS SKI

On day two or three of your tour along the Troll Trail, you'll make your way past the Spidsbergseter Resort Rondane. Stop here and go into the Aquavit Barn, built in the 1850s and stocked with more than 100 varieties of aquavit, a Scandinavian spirit distilled from grain or potato. The Barn also produces its own varietal, Fjøsaquavit, made with water from Rondane and spiced with local heather.

A skier looks to take a break in a log cabin at Rondane National Park.

KLOSTERS-SERNEUS

Must-Try Trail: Sertig Trail

MAX ELEVATION: 6,099 feet (1,859)   **AVERAGE SNOWFALL: 56 inches (142.2 cm)**
SKIABLE TERRAIN: 100+ miles (160.9+ km)   **OPEN SKI SEASON: November to March**

To most of the world, Davos is probably best known as the tony Swiss town where world business leaders gather each January at the World Economic Forum. But Davos, which is in eastern Switzerland's Landwasser Valley, along with the nearby town of Klosters, is also a cross-country skiing hub. In fact, the sport is taken so seriously here that the government employs a practice called "snow farming," in which a 2.5-mile (4 km) strip of trail is covered with sawdust at the end of the winter. This creates a refrigeration effect, preserving most of the snow throughout the warm summer months. In the fall, when the temperatures drop, the sawdust is removed and residents and tourists are able to enjoy skiing again well before there's enough snow to open the rest of the more than 100 miles (160.9 km) of trails (both classic ski trails and those groomed for skating). In the shadow of 10,000-foot (3,048 m) peaks, the extensive trail system wends through old farms, evergreen forests, and past icy rivers.

One of the most popular of those tracks is the Sertig Trail, an 11-mile (17.7 km) out-and-back that begins near the center of Davos and is as much a restaurant tour as it is a ski tour. From town, the groomed trail gradually climbs through the Sertig Valley, following the Sertig Brook past a sunny, open meadow to the east and a dense forest to the west. About a quarter of the

OPPOSITE: The Dischma valley offers more than 46 miles (74 km) of scenic cross-country trails and plenty of fresh snow.

PAGES 380-381: Walser-style houses speak to the traditional alpine architecture in the Davos area.

way up the valley is Restaurant Muhle Sertig, where you can enjoy a snack of dumplings and restore your electrolytes with a homemade Swiss version of Gatorade: *punsc,* which is hot water mixed with sugar and orange.

From here, the groomed trail ends and you're forced to break trail (classic skis are recommended) for 6.2 miles (10 km). You'll pass several hundred-year-old farmhouses and see milk cows milling about before making it to the top of the trail, where the valley opens up to expansive views of three toothy peaks: Mittagshorn, Plattenflue, and Hoch Ducan.

Here, you can treat yourself to a larger meal at the Walerhuss Sertig Restaurant, a quaint alpine chalet with a traditional Swiss menu, including fondue and veal with rosti (a potato pancake), and you can warm yourself up with a glass of local wine. Once you've had your fill of high alpine Swiss splendor, turn around and gently descend back into town.

OFF THE SLOPES

HC Davos, the town's local professional hockey team, has won Switzerland's National League title a record 31 times. Over the years big-name stars—including Joe Thornton, who also played for the Boston Bruins, and Jonas Hiller, who also played for the Anaheim Ducks—have skated for the team. The team plays at Vaillant Arena, a beautiful cathedral-like structure, and you can usually walk right up the night of a game and buy tickets.

SNOW FARM NZ

Must-Try Trail: Kirsty Burn

MAX ELEVATION: 6,445 feet (1,965 m) **AVERAGE SNOWFALL:** 200 inches (508 cm)
SKIABLE TERRAIN: 34.2 miles (55 km) **OPEN SKI SEASON:** June to September

Before Snow Farm became one of the premier cross-country skiing destinations in the world—the place where numerous elite Nordic ski racers decamp during New Zealand's winter to improve their skills—it was a sheep farm. When John Lee bought the property from his father in 1972, he thought that there might be a better use for the land than raising livestock. Substantial snowfall in the winter (the area averages some 200 inches/508 cm of snow between June and September) made farming difficult but could be great for recreation. "He loved the idea of cross-country skiing because he felt the baby boomers wouldn't be able to alpine ski for much longer, and he saw cross-country skiing as something older New Zealanders could do for fun," says Sam Lee, John Lee's son and the general manager of Snow Farm.

In the early 1980s, John Lee requested a land use change for the property, and in 1990 he opened Snow Farm, 6,329 acres (2,561 ha) of windswept, rolling, treeless hills with 34.2 miles (55 km) of well-groomed ski trails—wide lanes of corduroy that, other than fencing, are essentially the only disruption to the otherwise pristine fields of snow.

"It's one of the wildest landscapes you can imagine," says Simi Hamilton, a former athlete on the U.S. cross-country ski team. "You drive up from the valley floor—a 10-mile [16.1 km] drive through 35 switchbacks—and you're completely

OPPOSITE: Kirsty Burn offers leg-burning uphill climbs along its trail.

PAGES 384-385: Racers compete in the Freestyle Individual Ladies 5 km during the 2015 Winter Games in New Zealand.

above the tree line, surrounded by nothing but snow. It's some of the most optimal cross-country skiing terrain you can find anywhere."

The best of those trails is Kirsty Burn (also known as Kirtle Burn), a 6.2-mile (10 km) loop that starts at Snow Farm and crosses into the Pisa Conservation Area, more than 56,000 acres (22,662.4 ha) of wilderness. Because the trail meanders through the wilderness area, the Department of Conservation allows the Lees to groom it only five times each year. But hit on or around the time the grooming machine has laid down a fresh track, and it makes for a smooth, roller coaster–like ride through banked turns and waterfall descents.

When you ski it clockwise (the preferred route), the trail gently climbs along a plateau, a perfect vantage point for sweeping views of the Southern Alps, including Mount Aspiring, a nearly 10,000-foot (3,048 m) pyramidal peak. Upon reaching the top of Mount Pisa, 6,445 feet (1,964.4 m) above sea level, you'll descend through a drainage, past a small creek. "It's the best part of the trail," says Hamilton. "You're almost in these little slot canyons. It's fast and turny and incredibly fun."

WHERE TO STAY

The 50-bed Snow Farm Lodge, situated right next to the trails, is industrial looking and spartan. "It's nothing special, but it's clean and comfortable," says Hamilton. It offers a gym, wax room, bar, café, and restaurant that serves breakfast, lunch, and dinner. Often on the menu is a local specialty: mutton.

PROTECTING OUR WINTERS

When you finished the famous Vallée Blanche ski run on the Mer de Glace glacier in Chamonix in 1988, you simply clicked off your skis, walked up three steps, and were at the gondola. But since then, the glacier, which is the second biggest in France, has receded so much due to global warming that those three steps have become 600 to reach the gondola.

As skiers and snowboarders, we have the good fortune of seeing some of the world's most amazing corners: towering peaks, snow-dusted glades, an untouched backcountry terrain. These snowy wonderlands and epic pistes draw us back to the slopes again and again. And yet our winters are changing. Some places that never required snowmakers are now accumulating fewer and fewer inches of natural flakes, ski seasons are getting shorter, winter weather is getting warmer, and untouched terrain is becoming increasingly rare. It is our responsibility to protect these mountains before they're lost forever.

Skiers and snowboarders should be leading the charge to save our winters because we are in the privileged position of being able to see the changes taking place. It's our backyard and our responsibility. In 2007, professional snowboarder Jeremy Jones started Protect Our Winters (POW) as a community of 30,000, with snow-athlete ambassadors, looking to protect natural spaces in the world today. Their goal is to achieve carbon neutrality by 2050. You can find out more ways to help POW on its website: *protectourwinters.org*.

Not sure where to begin? Here are a few conservation guidelines to get you started:

1. **Vote.** This is an easy—and important—one. Vote for politicians who champion conservation, and let them (and their opponents) know why. Be vocal. Sign petitions. For as much good as we're doing individually, we need lawmakers to back it up on a global level.

2. **Support science.** Misinformation and choked-off funding are making scientific research difficult right when we need it the most. Whether it's a local grassroots project in your community, organizations looking at the larger picture, or solution-focused companies, you can provide support through donating your time, volunteering your individual expertise (be it graphic design or social media know-how), or backing them financially. You should also consider becoming citizen scientists by monitoring and documenting your surroundings on trips to the mountains and taking note of climate conditions.

3. **Drive less.** Get to your next slope via carpool or public transportation. According to the Environmental Protection Agency (EPA), America's transportation sector was responsible for 28 percent of greenhouse gas emissions in 2018. Pay attention to the transportation options that resorts offer you. Park City Mountain, for example, has a fleet of electric zero-emissions buses.

4. **Plant trees.** Plants help absorb carbon dioxide from the atmosphere and offset carbon emissions. In 2014, the EPA reported that the Land Use and Forestry Sector offset 11 percent of greenhouse gas emissions. Counteract the tree clearing that often comes along with trail building by planting your own trees or donating to organizations that do the work for you.

5. **Remember that plastic is not so fantastic.** In May 2018 National Geographic launched its Planet or Plastic? campaign, a multiyear effort to raise awareness about the global plastic crisis. A few fast plastic facts for you:

   - More than 40 percent of plastic is used once and then discarded, and 6.3 billion tons of plastic fill our landfills, landscapes, and oceans.

   - Nearly one million plastic bottles are sold every minute around the world.

   - Plastic takes nearly 400 years to degrade; a 2018 study found that only 9 percent of plastics are recycled.

Take active steps to reduce the plastic you use: Bring reusable water bottles with you, as well as multiuse utensils for lunch breaks. Oh, and skip the plastic straws, please. It's that simple. And effective.

SKIING AND SNOWBOARDING RESOURCES

There are a number of resources for skiers and snowboarders of all levels, whether you're looking for lift tickets, gear, the latest weather information, or travel tips. Here are just a few.

EPIC PASS
Under Vail Management, access more than 35 ski resorts and ski areas across the United States, Canada, and Australia through the Epic Pass. Use the affiliated *snow.com* website to plan your trips, with resort options, lift ticket choices, accommodation recommendations, and updated mountain conditions, and more. Vail Resorts is also dedicated to giving back with EpicPromise, an effort to ignite a passion for the outdoors while conserving the natural environment and local communities their ski destinations are built around.

IKON PASS
More than 40 ski resorts around the world—including in the United States, Canada, Japan, Australia, New Zealand, and Switzerland—can be accessed through the Ikon Pass under the Alterra Mountain Company umbrella. Use its website to buy lift tickets and make reservations and trip plans, and download the mobile app to maximize your time on the mountain.

THE MOUNTAIN COLLECTIVE
A Mountain Collective pass gives you two days of lift access to more than 20 premier ski destinations around the world in an international alliance of its partner resorts; that's more than 46 days of skiing for the year. The Mountain Collective also offers discounts for additional days at its partner ski resorts, special lodging deals, and suggested itinerary treks. There are no blackout dates under the pass.

CROSS COUNTRY SKI AREAS ASSOCIATION (CCSAA)

Use the CCSAA's directory of cross-country ski destinations around the United States and Canada to plan your next ski or snowshoe trip. Its website also includes the latest cross-country news, education tips, and recommended retailers for gear and equipment. A great bonus: When you buy new gear from participating retailers, you'll get three free visits to the CCSAA's participating ski and snowshoe areas using the Welcome Pass.

PROTECT OUR WINTERS (POW)

Founded in 2007 by professional snowboarder Jeremy Jones, POW is a community of athletes, scientists, creatives, and business leaders on a mission to protect our planet by achieving carbon neutrality by 2050. Targeting the outdoor community, POW looks to renewable energy, electric transportation, carbon pricing policies, and preventing fossil fuel extractions on public lands to make a difference. Their work helps guide outdoor enthusiasts to become climate advocates, helping to heal and preserve the spaces we love the most.

AVALANCHE EDUCATION AND TRAINING

Particularly for backcountry enthusiasts, avalanche education and training is the key to skiing and snowboarding safely. There are a number of resources where you can find information, take avalanche safety courses, and continue your avalanche training and education. The American Avalanche Association is a nonprofit organization dedicated to education, professional development, outreach, and research; the American Avalanche Institute has offered a systemic approach to backcountry travel since 1974; and the American Institute for Avalanche Research and Education (AIARE), established in 1998, offers research-based professional and recreational avalanche training to those in the United States, South America, and Europe.

SEASONWORKERS

Looking to make a living on the slopes? You can have your snow and ski it too. For seasonal job opportunities at ski areas around the world, look to *seasonworkers.com* for the latest job listings and application tools—with opportunities for ski and snowboard instructor positions, ski patrols, lift operations, and more.

SLOPES BY COUNTRY

ACKNOWLEDGMENTS

If I'd not been so lucky to grow up skiing, I would not have had the knowledge, connections, and expertise needed to write this book. For that, I thank my parents, who taught me how to ski and helped cultivate my love for the sport. Special thanks goes to Tess Weaver, whose help and support throughout the writing of this book were of immeasurable importance; Nicole Gull McElroy, who helped with research; and Lindsey Vonn, one of the great ski racers of all time, who was generous enough to write the foreword for this book.

This book would not have been possible without the help of experts, including ski resort staffers, guides, instructors, patrollers, professional skiers and snowboarders, and numerous others. Thanks to all of you who took the time to speak with me for this project.

Nor would this book exist without the hard-working staff at National Geographic. A very big thank-you goes to Allyson Johnson, my very patient editor, as well as art director Sanaa Akkach, senior photo editor Adrian Coakley, photo editor Charlie Borst, production editor Judith Klein, and the public relations and marketing team of Daneen Goodwin, Ann Day, and Kelly Forsythe.

Finally, I acknowledge my ski partners—the people who regularly bang around on chairlifts with me, join me on backcountry ski tours, and help keep me safe. Thank you Tess, Mark, Mary Ann, Andy, Josh, Karen, Damon, Phil, Lindsay, Pace, Tracy, Kristan, Erin, Kim, Joel, Charlotte, and Steven, as well as Alison, Rogan, and Johnny (my original ski partners). Let's never stop skiing together.

ABOUT THE AUTHOR

GORDY MEGROZ is a freelance writer and contributing editor for *Outside* magazine, for which he writes investigative pieces, as well as profiles of athletes, companies, and places. His work has also appeared in *Wired, Men's Journal, Bloomberg Businessweek*, and *SKI*. Megroz was born and raised in Vermont and now lives in Jackson, Wyoming. When he's not at his desk, you can find him skiing, mountain biking, or climbing around the Tetons.

Four-time Olympian **LINDSEY VONN** (Foreword) brought her sporting career to an end on February 10, 2019, after competing at her eighth World Championship in Åre, Sweden, and taking home the bronze in the downhill event. During the 19 years she competed at the highest level, she established herself as the greatest female skier of all time, setting records including becoming the first ever U.S. women's downhill Olympic champion, an unmatched 82 World Cup victories, 20 crystal globes, and 43 downhill wins.

ILLUSTRATIONS CREDITS

Cover, Grant Gunderson; Back cover, Ming T. Poon; 2-3, Christian Pondella; 4-5, Mattias Fredriksson; 7, Martin Bernetti/AFP via Getty Images; 9, Matías Donoso/La Parva; 10-11, Ben Bloom/Getty Images; 12-13, Adventure_Photo/Getty Images; 15, Joshua Esquivel; 17, Chip Kalback; 19, Scott Markewitz; 20-21, Chris McLennan/Alamy Stock Photo; 22, miralex/Getty Images; 23, Jack Affleck/Vail Resorts; 25, Sofia Jaramillo; 26-7, Kennan Harvey/Cavan Images; 29, Tony Demin/Cavan Images; 30-31, David L. Moore - US West/Alamy Stock Photo; 33, Don Hammond/Getty Images; 34-5, John Russell/ Photo Resource Hawaii/Alamy Stock Photo; 37, Steve Smith/Getty Images; 39, Chris Bennett/ Cavan Images; 41, Craig Moore/Cavan Images; 42-3, Craig Moore/Cavan Images; 45, Jeffrey Murray/ Cavan Images; 47, Jordan Lutes/Cavan Images; 48-9, Brian Stevenson/robertharding.com; 50, George Ostertag/Alamy Stock Photo; 51, John Gress/Corbis via Getty Images; 53, Brown W Cannon III/Alamy Stock Photo; 54-5, stellamc/Alamy Stock Photo; 57, Patrick Frilet/hemis.fr/Alamy Stock Photo; 59, Topher Donahue/Cavan Images; 61, Randy Lincks/ Alamy Stock Photo; 63, Ian Dagnall/Alamy Stock Photo; 64-5, Menno Boermans/Cavan Images; 66, Menno Boermans/Cavan Images; 67, Francois Roux /Alamy Stock Photo; 69, Flaviu Boerescu/ Alamy Stock Photo; 70-71, Ian Dagnall/Alamy Stock Photo; 72, Hans-Werner Rodrian/imageBROKER/ Alamy Stock Photo; 73, Moreno Geremetta/ mauritius images GmbH/Alamy Stock Photo; 75, Mark Upfield/Alamy Stock Photo; 77, Yuri Smityuk/ TASS; 78-9, Alexander Piragis/Getty Images; 81, Scottish Viewpoint/Alamy Stock Photo; 83, Aljaž Sedovšek/www.visitmaribor.si; 84-5, Dejan Bulut/ www.visitmaribor.si; 87, Scott Markewitz; 88-9, Prisma/Christof Sonderegger/Alamy Stock Photo; 90, Stefano Politi Markovina/Alamy Stock Photo; 91, PatitucciPhoto/Cavan Images; 93, Damiano Levati/Cavan Images; 94-5, Oliver Förstner/ Alamy Stock Photo; 96, VogelSP/Alamy Stock Photo; 97, Mario Colonel/Cavan Images; 99, Ben Girardi/Cavan Images; 101, Travel Collection/ Image Professionals GmbH/Alamy Stock Photo; 102-103, Scott Serfas; 105, Marcel Rabelo/Alamy Stock Photo; 107, Anton Sponar; 108-109, Anton Sponar; 111, Menno Boermans/Cavan Images; 112-13, Wolfgang Kaehler/LightRocket via Getty Images; 114, Avalon/Universal Images Group via Getty Images; 115, Aliaksandra Ivanova/EyeEm/Getty Images; 117, Gavriel Jecan/age fotostock/Alamy Stock Photo; 119, Tomohiro Ohsumi/Bloomberg via Getty Images; 121, Adam Kroenert; 123, Clive Weston; 125, Peter Unger/Getty Images; 126-7,

Since 1888, the National Geographic Society has funded more than 14,000 research, conservation, education, and storytelling projects around the world. National Geographic Partners distributes a portion of the funds it receives from your purchase to National Geographic Society to support programs including the conservation of animals and their habitats.

Get closer to National Geographic Explorers and photographers, and connect with our global community. Join us today at nationalgeographic.com/join

For rights or permissions inquiries, please contact National Geographic Books Subsidiary Rights: bookrights@natgeo.com

ISBN: 978-1-4262-2195-8

Printed in Malaysia

21/QRM/1

The information in this book has been carefully checked and to the best of our knowledge is accurate. However, details are subject to change, and the publisher cannot be responsible for such changes, or for errors or omissions. Assessments of sites, hotels, and restaurants are based on the author's subjective opinions, which do not necessarily reflect the publisher's opinion.

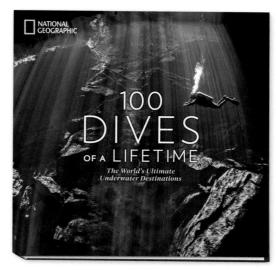
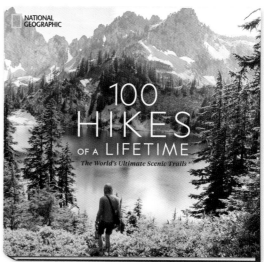